THE COCKROACH
COMBAT MANUAL II

Dr. Austin M. Frishman & Paul J. Bello

AuthorHouse™
1663 Liberty Drive
Bloomington, IN 47403
www.authorhouse.com
Phone: 1-800-839-8640

© 2013 Dr. Austin M. Frishman & Paul J. Bello. All rights reserved.

No part of this book may be reproduced, stored in a retrieval system, or transmitted by any means without the written permission of the author.

Published by AuthorHouse 10/23/2013

ISBN: 978-1-4918-2065-0 (e)
ISBN: 978-1-4918-2064-3 (sc)

Library of Congress Control Number: 2013918461

Certain stock imagery © Thinkstock.
Any people depicted in stock imagery provided by Thinkstock are models, and such images are being used for illustrative purposes only.

This book is printed on acid-free paper.

Because of the dynamic nature of the Internet, any web addresses or links contained in this book may have changed since publication and may no longer be valid. The views expressed in this work are solely those of the author and do not necessarily reflect the views of the publisher, and the publisher hereby disclaims any responsibility for them.

Dedications:

PHOTO 0.1: **Dr. Austin M. Frisham and Mrs. Barbara Frishman**

This book is dedicated to Barbara Frishman, my wife of more than fifty years, a true partner in every sense of the word. She has been my right and left hand since day one. Thank you for being by my side in our personal and business lives. No one could be happier.
—Austin M. Frishman

PHOTO 0.2: **Nicholas M. Bello, US Army Air Corp.**

PHOTO 0.3: **Nicholas and Phyllis Bello, 1942.**

PHOTO 0.4: **Nicholas, Anthony, and Mary Ann with Mom and Dad, July 2012.**

This book is dedicated to my Mom and Dad. On November 13, 2012, just before Thanksgiving, we lost my dad. He was a WW II B-17 veteran. Mom and Dad were married sixty-five years. They did their very best to raise a family of five children, we know they had their hands full and we can't thank them enough.
—Paul Bello

Contents

Why This Book? 1

Foreword 3

Chapter 1   The Evolution and History of Cockroaches 4

Chapter 2   Cockroach Biology, Development, and Behavior 9

Chapter 3   Cockroach Identification, Inspection, and Detection 18

Chapter 4   Diseases and Damage Associated with Cockroaches 25

Chapter 5   Cockroach Inspection and Detection 30

Chapter 6   Cockroach Trivia and Records, Unusual Circumstances, and Worst-Case Scenarios 39

Chapter 7   Non-Chemical Cockroach Control Methodologies and IPM 52

Chapter 8   Insecticides, Resistance, and Cockroach Baits 60

Chapter 9   Killing Cockroaches with Insecticides 77

Chapter 10   Application Equipment Use and Care 85

Chapter 11   Special Situations 91

Chapter 12   Solving Cockroach Problems 102

Chapter 13   Frequently-Asked Questions 108

Appendix I: "Classic Frishman" 119

     "The Top 100 Best Cockroach Control Tips" 120

     "Typical Pests Found in and around Health-Care Facilities" 124

     "25 Key Points When Writing Pest Control Contracts for Health-Care Facilities" 125

     "Domestic Cockroaches and Human Bacterial Diseases." 128

     "Twelve Ways to Read a Sticky Trap." 129

     "Are Baits the Silver Bullet of Cockroach Control?" 130

"Are You Using Sticky Traps the Right Way?" 131

"The American Roach—High-Rise Headache." 132

"How to Improve Cockroach Bait Application." 133

"Questions to Ask before Treating an Office Building." 134

"Death, Taxes, and Cockroach Infestations." 135

"Control from the Cockroach's Perspective." 136

Appendix II: Cockroach Bait Aversion Q&A 137

Appendix III: Sponsors 141

Appendix IV: Acknowledgments, References, and Resources 163

Appendix V: About the Authors 167

Editor's Note:

Terminology, phraseology, and industry slang used on a daily basis vary from city to city, region to region, company to company, and technician to technician. Cockroaches are known by many names across the world. Entomology wise, it is proper to call them "cockroaches"; however, our chosen words vary. Many city folks in the northeast seem to add a vowel sound to the word and call them *"cock-ah-roaches"*. Some of us simply call them roaches, perhaps because it's quicker. Is either of these slang terms entomologically correct? No. In this book you'll see use of the word "roach" or "roaches." We trust the reader will understand.

Unless otherwise noted, all photos are copyright Paul J. Bello.

Illustrations are by Aubry C. Leal, Aubry Leal Art Studios, Johns Creek, GA

Why This Book?

The original *Cockroach Combat Manual* published in 1980 was written by Dr. Frishman and Arthur Schwartz. In those days the cockroach was the number one pest, and cockroach cleanout work was conducted on a daily basis by many of the pest professional companies in the New York metropolitan area. In that area, where many Frishman students were introduced to the pest management industry, some of us did multiple cockroach cleanouts per day.

Ah, the good old days of cockroach cleanouts—where roaches crawled up our pants legs, fell from the ceiling on our heads, and found their way into our shirts as we worked. Cockroach cleanouts—where you smelled the roaches before the customer opened the door. Cockroach cleanouts—where live roaches hid in the door jam and molding on the *outside* of the apartment door. Cockroach cleanouts—where young children had their eyebrows and eyelashes clipped off by roaches as they slept.

Much has changed since then. Those of us with more than thirty years of industry experience have observed these changes. A photo of my pest technician's toolbox taken back in the 1970s would be remarkably different from a similar photo taken in 2013. In fact, nearly the *only* thing that would be the same in such a photo would likely be the toolbox itself.

Just for fun, I wondered how a conversation might go at the next industry meeting, when a new technician might ask, "What was it like back then to do a cockroach cleanout?" My reply might go something like this: "Well, you wouldn't believe it. We had equipment, we had chemicals, and we had roaches up the wazzoo. Baits? We didn't have baits. We had ULV foggers, and we slaughtered roaches by the thousands on a daily basis. We had the *good stuff*, we had chlorinated hydrocarbons, we had organophosphates, we had carbamates, and resistance was either a rumor or a weak excuse for not doing good work." Ah, the good old days indeed.

—Paul J. Bello, President
PJB Pest Management Consulting

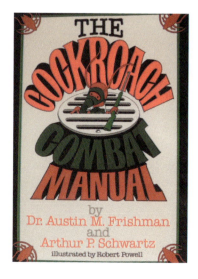

PHOTO 0.6. **The original *Cockroach Combat Manual* was published in 1980 and written by Dr. Austin M. Frishman and Arthur Schwartz.**

For more than fifty years I have dedicated much of my life to combating cockroaches as a point man in the field and while attempting to train others in the classroom. It is time to compile and condense my observations, experience, and knowledge into one source so that others can benefit from this information in the eternal battle between man and cockroaches. The contents of this book, however, will equally benefit pest-management technicians, their customers, the victims with the cockroach problems, and the curious.

—Dr. Austin M. Frishman, President
AMF Pest Management Services, Inc.

These days we still have cockroach problems, but things have dramatically changed. The materials have changed, the equipment has changed, the technicians have changed, the customers have changed, and the cockroaches have changed. In this book, we provide the reader with information and practical tips with which to successfully address these differences.

We hope you find the *Cockroach Combat Manual II* a welcome and useful addition to your pest management knowledge base and arsenal.

Yours in pest management,
Dr. Austin M. Frishman and Paul J. Bello

Foreword
By Dr. William D. McClellan, Ph. D.

The urban cockroach market is and will continue to provide challenging situations for controlling cockroaches. The market is full of many diverse products and methods. How to incorporate these various tools to resolve cockroach problems is the focus of this book.

Cockroaches are one of the most studied insect species in the urban environment and are known to have been present on this planet for over 300 million years. They have the well-earned reputation of being one of the most adaptable and successful insect groups to inhabit this planet. The development of control strategies using the latest technological advances and research knowledge are essential to the successful management of these pests.

The control of cockroaches in the urban environment has evolved significantly over the last 30 years. The development of resistant cockroach populations is an important industry consideration for control strategies. It is important that the pest professional has the latest information available in developing control programs for their customers.

Over the years I have had the privilege of working with both Dr. Austin Frishman and Paul Bello when I was the Technical Manager of Zeneca Professional Products (now Syngenta). I asked Austin to review a presentation that I was making to NPMA when I first joined Zeneca. He offered me guidance and advice that have remained with me to this day. He is one of the icons in the industry who learns, teaches and provides leadership. He is involved with the issues of importance to the technician, to the PMP, business leaders, to the PMP customers and to policy issues at the local and national level. He remains a very important mentor to me.

Paul Bello and I first worked together in Zeneca Professional Products. Over the years I have developed an understanding and respect for the passion and dedication he has for learning, teaching, training and his excellent problem solving skills within the Pest Management Industry. Paul is a former student of Austin Frishman and has what Dr Frishman refers to as a "unique quality of extensive hands on field experience". Both Austin Frishman and Paul Bello are qualified experts in this field. They have extensive knowledge and experience with each being a recognized as a technical experts and industry consultants.

In **The Cockroach Combat Manual II** Austin Frishman and Paul Bello have combined to provide a valuable and up to date resource for training, reference and practical management of cockroach populations in the urban environment. This book should be of interest to pest professionals, researchers, regulatory authorities and to the lay public. It is an informative and interesting read covering the many issues and challenges confronting the management of cockroach populations in the urban environment.

Dr. William D. McClellan, Ph.D., President
McClellan Inc., Pawlet, VT

Chapter 1

The Evolution and History of Cockroaches

Three hundred and fifty million years ago, cockroaches thrived. This age was called the Carboniferous Period. Scientists refer to it as the *age of the cockroaches* because at that time, these insects had reached their peak in number of species as well as the abundance of each species. The presence of a warm, moist environment allowed these cockroaches to dominate the world at that time, yet today none of these species exist. However, the current-day species that evolved from this extinct group are called Paleoblattidae.

"Blattidae" is the Latin term used to describe present-day cockroaches, and the word "paleo" refers to the term "ancient." The Carboniferous period came toward the end of the Paleozoic Era, which began about five hundred million years ago and ended two hundred million years ago. Dinosaurs had not yet begun to roam the earth. As early *Homo sapiens* evolved from between four hundred thousand and two hundred fifty thousand years ago, cockroaches predate man's arrival by more than three hundred million years.

Some experts recognize twelve families of fossil cockroaches. The largest family is called the Archimylacris and is comprised of as many as 350 species. Surprisingly, fossil remains indicate that there have been very few structural changes in cockroaches. The shape of the cockroach bodies and their fondness for living in moist places has changed little over these many years. Domestic cockroaches that exist today have evolved to the point where they can withstand drier conditions. Their wings have become reduced in size, and their eggs are now deposited in a protective capsule to reduce dehydration. Primitive cockroaches would have deposited their eggs singly in a moist environment.

The sword-shaped ovipositor evolved over a period of time to be retracted into the abdomen of the male cockroach and into the formation of a genital pouch in the female. In the primitive period, the function of the ovipositor was to inject eggs into the soil or other suitable media. Today the ovipositor is used to guide eggs into the ootheca, an egg capsule that houses the individual eggs and is produced by the adult female. Of the domestic cockroaches, with the exception of the German cockroach, the egg capsule is dropped or

PHOTO 1.1: **A current-day cockroach egg capsule.**

affixed to various surfaces by the adult female. This waterproof structure protects the eggs during development of the nymph within and further allows these creatures to encroach upon man.

There are two main locations in North America where scientists collect fossil cockroaches: the middle or lower measures of Illinois, and the upper coal measures in Kansas.

Having inhabited the Earth for hundreds of millions of years before humans were present, it behooves us to start when "we humans" entered the historical picture. About seventy thousand years ago modern humans were dwelling in the Middle East and Northern Africa whilst Neanderthals were running around Europe and Western Asia. It took about fifteen to twenty thousand years for our ancestors to become the dominant species—a mere speck compared to the ubiquitous cockroach, which had already been here for about three hundred and fifty million years prior to early man.

Probably from day one cockroaches were uninvited guests and have managed to remain uninvited guests throughout time. Household cockroaches are as ancient as the concept of food within the home. Those of us who have these pests within our home are simply following a time-honored tradition and precedent. So if you have them, don't be too upset.

PHOTO 1.2: **A fossilized cockroach from millions of years ago.**

It is believed that the four major household species all came to North America from Africa. Some made the roundabout trip through the Middle East to Europe in trade caravans, or across the Mediterranean in Greek and Phoenician ships, arriving centuries later in North America. Others traveled directly across the Atlantic in early explorer and slave ships. This latter group included the so-called American cockroach (*Periplaneta americana*).

References to the cockroach prevail through history. Pedanius Dioscorides, a Greek who was an army physician for the Emperor Nero stated in the first century that cockroach entrails, when mixed with oil and stuffed into the ear, would cure earaches. This information was included in his treatise on medicine called the *De Materia Medica*. For sixteen centuries, *De Materia Medica* was considered the highest authority on medicine and was universally studied by medical students and botanists.

The cockroach is also mentioned in another first-century manuscript, a scientific encyclopedia called *Natural History*. Written by Pliny the Elder, it contained almost the same recipe for earaches as that of Dioscorides's but slightly improved: the oil that was mixed with the cockroaches had to be rose oil. To Pliny, a naturalist, cockroaches were a cure-all. When crushed, he observed, they would cure itching, tumors, and scabs; when ingested with their wings and feet cut off, they relieved swollen glands.

As noted earlier, cockroaches were amongst the original travelers on sailing ships. Cockroaches at sea are described in the Danish navy annals of 1611 AD. From time to time, apparently, cockroach hunts were held. The price for a thousand cockroaches was a bottle of brandy from the cook's locked pantry. Cockroach time was party time in those days. The navy annals record a single catch of this sort bringing in 32,500 cockroaches.

The Spanish Armada had the same problems. Sir Francis Drake reported that upon capturing the *San Felipe*, his boarding party found the bombarded decks overrun with cockroaches. Cockroaches aboard ships have always manifested themselves in unpleasant ways. For instance, R. H. Lewis wrote that "on a voyage from England to Tasmania, hundreds of cockroaches were flying around my cabin. They were in immense confusion and had a communication with every part of the ship, between the timbers or the skin. The ravages they committed on every edible item were very extensive. Not a biscuit but was more or less polluted by them, and amongst the cargo of three hundred cases of cheese, which had holes in them to prevent their sweating, were considerably damaged, some of them being half-devoured and not one without some marks of their residence."

British entomologist A. Nichols, among others, reported sailors frequently complained of having their toenails, fingernails, and calloused parts of their hands and feet nibbled on by cockroaches. Also reported was the consumption of eyelashes and hair from sleeping crews and passengers, especially children.

Caudell, another entomologist on an explorer's expedition to British Columbia, reported: "On this trip I had them served to me in three different styles. Alive in strawberries, a la carte with fried fish—and baked in a biscuit."

As late as the sixteenth century, physicians were still prescribing cockroach entrails as an excellent remedy for sore ears. A Viennese physician by the name of Tatthiold updated Dioscorides's recipe of sixteen hundred years earlier; the cockroach entrails had to be cooked in oil instead of just mixed. In 1725, Jamaican children were still being fed cockroaches as a worm cure. The fact is, reports of cockroaches being used medicinally and nutritionally persist around the world even today.

In the summer of 1979, more than a million German cockroaches were found thriving in a two-family house in Schenectady, New York. T-shirts were quickly distributed with the words "Schenectady—Cockroach Capital of the World."

CHAPTER 1: THE EVOLUTION AND HISTORY OF COCKROACHES

The cockroach has frequently been a social issue. In Northern Germany it is referred to as "Schwwabe," a term for inhabitants of Southern Germany. In the south the cockroach is popularly known as "Preusze," after the northern Germans. This species of cockroach is known in the United States even today among pest management professionals as the German cockroach. The names "Yankee Settler," "Croton Bug," and "Bombay Canary," to name a few, have also been used at one time or another for this cockroach.

Cockroach history would not be complete without mentioning its debut in the legal profession. Fifty years ago a renowned Danish baker was faced with a trial when a customer found a cockroach in a piece of pastry. The baker, visualizing the end of his career, asked the court to see the piece of evidence. It was handed to him and he exclaimed, "Cockroach? That is not a cockroach, that is a raisin …" and he then swallowed it. He was acquitted.

What is it about the cockroach that makes it objectionable to human beings? Is it simply an aesthetic inconvenience? We know that eradication attempts have been made throughout the ages. For instance, Captain William Bligh, in his 1792 chronicling of the voyages of the *HMS Bounty*, described his attempts to rid the ship of cockroaches using boiling water.

W. S. Blatchley described the following common methods used in Mexico: "To get rid of cockroaches—catch three and put them in a bottle, and so carry them to where two roads cross. Here hold the bottle upside down, and as they fall out repeat aloud three credos. Than all the cockroaches in the house from which these three came will go away."

As late as 1905 the Japanese navy was still using the seventeenth-century Danish method of eradication. They called it "Shore Leave for Cockroaches." A Japanese seaman would only have to capture three hundred cockroaches to be granted a day's shore leave. With characteristic succinctness and aplomb, the Japanese described the purpose as follows: "To promote extermination of cockroaches in a warship because, on the one hand, any warship suffers from numerous cockroaches, and on the other hand, any seaman likes shore leave."

Cockroaches are objectionable for more than aesthetic reasons. Aside from their being unwelcome visitors of minute size, great numbers, unpredictable direction, and speed of flight, cockroaches happen to be contaminators of food supplies. If you have never smelled their odor, you are lucky. Called "attar of roaches," it is the combined product of their excrement, of fluid exuded from their abdominal scent glands, and of a dark-colored fluid regurgitated from their mouths while feeding. This attar fouls food.

The dominant cockroach today is the German cockroach, or *Blatella Germanica* (Linnaeus). Originally this cockroach evolved in North Africa. It is believed to have migrated to eastern Europe in Greek and Phoenician ships, whereby it then spread to Asia Minor, the Black Sea region, and southern Russia. According to P. B. Cornwell, a British entomologist and director of research for Rentokil Laboratories Ltd., East Gunstead, Sussex, England, this species then spread northward and westward across Europe. Once entrenched in western Europe, it was then just a matter of time before the German cockroach successfully invaded ships. Today these world travelers go first class via planes, ships, trains, and buses. The three main factors that contribute to the dominance of the German cockroach are its small size, short life cycle, and prolific breeding capabilities.

Over the centuries, individual roaches within a given species mutate. Environmental conditions determine which mutants are selected to survive. Cockroaches have exhibited an extraordinary record of successes, including the ability to develop resistance to pesticides, withstand high dosages of radiation, and survive on a minimal food intake.

New Invading Species

Cockroaches are true survivors and successful invaders due to their ability to turn up nearly anywhere via introduction due to various forms of commerce and transport. As an example, years ago tropical species such as the Surniam cockroach became problematic within structures such as shopping malls in the northeast, where decorative potted tropical plants were placed. Thriving quite nicely within the soil of these potted plants, interior plant-scape suppliers unknowingly delivered this roach problem to their customers.

Even as this book goes to print, the probability of a new invasive cockroach species is very much a reality. In 2013, technicians working at Bell Environmental Services collected a new species of cockroach in New York City. Using DNA analysis and morphological features, this species was confirmed. The species *Periplaneta japonica* was identified and confirmed at the Rutgers University, the State University of New Jersey, Department of Entomology. These cockroaches were found at the exterior of a building beneath various plantings and were able to survive outdoors over the cold New York winter. They were not buried in the soil but were found around stones and planting materials.

PHOTO 1.3: **This unusual but attractive roach is the pale-bordered field cockroach. It was collected on a hospital rooftop in the metro Atlanta area but is not a structural pest.**

Chapter 2
Cockroach Biology, Development, and Behavior

Fossilized cockroaches show no great differences from present-day species, and today's cockroaches doubtlessly live much the same way as their ancestors more than a billion generations ago. The fact that they still exist after such a long time, let alone that they are basically unchanged, is a magnificent tribute to the success of their design and structure. The cockroach is a grandly simple creature. They are living fossils, unencumbered by sophisticated evolutionary amenities such as lungs, reliance on vision, and discriminatory taste.

The basic domestic cockroach ranges in color from yellowish tan to brownish black and in size from one-half inch to one-and-one-half inches. It is not slimy but is covered with a hard, waxy coating. Like all insects, it has a three-part body: head, thorax, and abdomen. However, you never see the three parts, not even the head, unless the cockroach is dead and happens to be lying on its back. This is because its wings cover the entire back, and its head is bowed downward under a protective crown, the pronotum, with the mouth projecting backward between its front legs. Therefore, you mainly see the back, legs, and antennae sticking out, and maybe the cerci on the rear end. Pointy spines project from the legs of the cockroach. The legs and wings, if present, rise from the thorax.

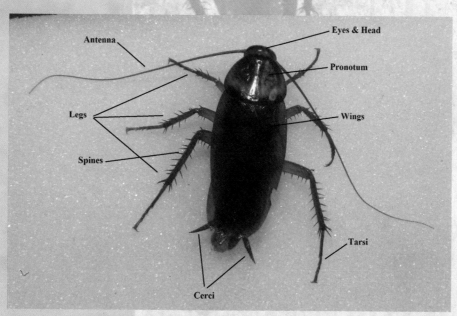

PHOTO 2.1: **American cockroach with some body parts indicated.**

The cockroach does most of its sensing by picking up vibrations in the air, essentially hearing or feeling movements of its antennae on one end and the cerci on the other. The antennae can also smell things. The cerci serve a sensory function. These two hair-covered appendages project from the posterior end of the cockroach. Sensory nerves of the cerci are directly connected to six long, slender, and powerful legs, bypassing the brain. When the cockroach "feels" a threat presence anywhere in the room (when you speak a word, take a breath, or take a step) it doesn't even think about it, its legs start moving first (see photo 2.2).

Evolution has favored the shortening of the evasive behavior responses of the cockroach to the point where its reaction time is limited only by the speed of the neural impulses down the nerves from the cerci to the legs (this reaction time has been measured by researchers). If you ever observe a cockroach standing still with its cerci sticking up in the air, you'll know it's checking things out. There is no way you can get near a cockroach unless it starts running and can't find a place to hide. This is a rarity for a cockroach because its body is built of flattened plates with the legs sticking out horizontally. Constructed this way allows the roach to slip into surprisingly small and tiny cracks that you couldn't get a match into. It will also use its wings if properly disturbed.

PHOTO 2.2: **The cerci are sensory structures located near the tip of the cockroach abdomen.**

A cockroach needs very little to survive. A little warmth, a little shelter, a little moisture, and a small amount of food are all that is required for a cockroach to survive. Although it prefers starchy foods such as bread, potatoes, apples, and beer, it will eat anything. The cockroach is not capable of biting; rather, it scrapes and chews or munches. It will as soon snack on paper and soiled clothing as on scattered crumbs. It seeks high humidity and warm temperatures. It tries to avoid light and prefers to hide in cracks and crevices. A cockroach is extraordinarily hardy. It will survive the loss of legs and antennae. It will withstand temperatures from 10 to 130 degrees Fahrenheit for short periods, in addition to depressurization.

A cockroach can go for long periods of time without food or water. While it lives and breeds in close proximity to its food supply, it will wander, forage, and even migrate if need be in search of food. But in reality, it doesn't take much to keep a cockroach fat and happy.

Cockroaches come in four basic "flavors": male, female, nymph, and egg. The male is thin and slender with a tapered rear end, whereas the female is stout and robust with bulbous hindquarters. The nymph is simply the stage between hatching and maturity. Cockroaches develop by gradual metamorphosis, and nymphal cockroaches resemble the adults.

Cockroaches are highly prolific; the female is essentially a fertile breeding machine. Although the time may vary among different species, and environmental factors play a part, it is just a matter of days between reaching maturity and producing the first batch of eggs. Cockroaches need only mate once in their lives to produce many batches of fertile offspring; however, they are known to do it again and again anyway. Incidentally, some cockroaches can and will reproduce parthenogenetically—that is, without any mating or male intervention. Such eggs laid by females give rise to new generations consisting of only females. Perhaps a word here for "cockroach lib"?

Cockroaches always hatch from egg capsules, little bean-shaped cases in which baby cockroaches are stacked side by side like coins. In some species, such as the German cockroach, the female carries the egg capsule protruding from her posterior until the babies are ready to hatch. Other species deposit the capsule as soon as it is formed. Spotting a viable egg capsule is worse than spotting a real live cockroach because with the egg capsule, you are looking at from sixteen to more than forty potential cockroaches in your house compared to just one.

Newly hatched cockroaches are called nymphs. Some of the differences between a nymph and an adult, other than size, is that the nymph doesn't have wings or a few other things you cannot see, such as genitalia. The nymph also does not have the distinct markings that the adult of the species has.

Cockroaches develop through gradual metamorphosis, and the nymphs resemble the adults (see photo 2.3). The way a nymph eventually becomes an adult is through molting, which is the shedding of one skin for a new one. A cockroach's skin is actually its exoskeleton. A nymph cockroach molts by breathing, taking in air until it bursts its own skin. The cockroach's skin also happens to be its exoskeleton. The exoskeleton splits right down the middle and the nymph squirms out, this time a little larger than its previous size.

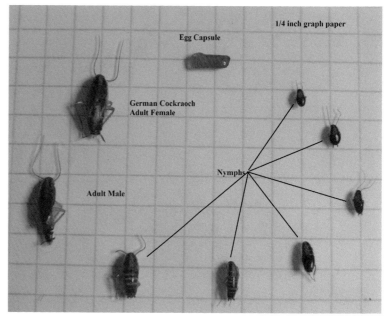

PHOTO 2.3: **German cockroach life cycle from egg capsule to adult.**

After their initial hatching, cockroach nymphs may molt from six to a dozen times before they become adults. This varies by species. If a nymph should happen to lose any appendage during this time, it will generate another in a subsequent molt. Occasionally a pest professional will hear reports of an albino cockroach. Any stories about albino cockroaches you've heard are simply observations of newly molted nymphs, which are white. They shortly turn dark with exposure to the air. Don't feel bad if you've been fooled by these white cockroaches because, apparently, their fellow cockroaches don't recognize them either, as these albino nymphs are highly susceptible to cannibalism until they darken.

Cockroaches are predictable when living in their own element and with no extraordinary stress. The more we learn about how they behave, the easier it is to work on management strategies to eliminate them.

They possess a few disgusting habits. The very immature feed on the feces of the adults, a behavior called carprophagy. Cockroaches will also feed on the carcasses of other dead cockroaches, a behavior called necrophagy. They will also feed on the vomitus from other cockroaches, a behavior known as emetophagy. These disgusting habits contribute to the success of our modern-day cockroach baits to work so well in our cockroach management program efforts because due to these feeding behaviors, there are multiple opportunities for cockroaches to ingest bait products.

Once German cockroaches establish a population, they establish a "trail" to help newly developed members find food and water. These trails are made with chemical signals known as pheromones. There are also pheromones or chemical signals that let cockroaches know where the best hiding spots, or harborages, are located. These pheromones may soon lead us to even better bait and other control-product developments in the future.

PHOTO 2.4: **Cockroaches can deposit great quantities of fecal matter, such as here in a kitchen cabinet. Immature roaches feed on such fecal matter, a behavior known as carprophagy.**

If you are going to battle with any adversary, it helps to know their strengths and weaknesses. It is no different when you tackle a German cockroach population on your premises. Below is a list of German cockroach strengths:

Cryptic—They hide most of the time, spending from 70 to 95 percent of their time in their harborages, which are tiny cracks, crevices, and hidden voids. Like other insect pests, cockroaches are cryptobiotic creatures, carrying on their day-to-day lives in a hidden world.

Nocturnal—They prefer darkness and are most active at night when we are not.

Domestic—They thrive best in close proximity to man within our structures. They take advantage of the various opportunities we afford them through our own habits.

CHAPTER 2: COCKROACH BIOLOGY, DEVELOPMENT, AND BEHAVIOR

Small—Their small size and flattened body enable them to hide in an incredible number of locations, even in the insulating liner of your refrigerator door.

Fast—They run fast enough to avoid being caught and often elude detection. By the time your shoe hits the floor, they are often gone. Contrary to popular belief, pointed shoes will not help.

Sticky Pads—Cockroaches such as the German and American cockroach have sticky pads on the tarsi, which enable them to climb smooth surfaces including glass and stainless steel, thus providing them unlimited access and travel and escape routes (see photo 2.5).

High Reproductive Capability—They are the most prolific of all domestic cockroaches. Popping out about forty offspring per month, a female German cockroach can give rise to a surprising number of offspring. Even if you kill 90 percent of the cockroaches every month, it would not put a dent in the total number still present.

Carry Their Egg Capsule with Them—By protecting their young in a water-resistant capsule and carrying it with them until ready to hatch, predators and parasites have little chance to reach the next generation of German cockroach. Most other species of cockroaches deposit their egg capsules and leave them vulnerable to attack from various entities.

PHOTO 2.5: **Cockroach tarsi are equipped with sticky pads that enable them to climb smooth surfaces.** Photo courtesy of Dr. Phil Koehler, University of Florida, Department of Entomology.

Opportunistic and Adaptable—As soon as you come up with a new cockroach control gadget, they find out how to live in it. This includes smoke detectors, electronics, and stored newspaper.

Genetically Resilient to Inbreeding—Even in the laboratory you can keep generation after generation alive starting from a single female.

Armed with a Host of Defense Mechanisms—The German cockroaches have early warning detectors

PHOTO 2.6: **By carrying the egg case until it's time to hatch, the German cockroach female serves to protect her unborn young from hazards including predators and pesticides.**

that enable them to respond to threats and dangers quickly to escape. They have long antennae, sensory hairs, and cerci on the posterior to keep them "on their toes" and aware of their surroundings at all times.

Ability to Withstand Temperature Extremes—They can make it at just above freezing to almost one hundred degrees Fahrenheit. They do well in temperature ranges from the mid 70s to 80s, which happens to be about the same temperature range that we keep our homes. However, their optimal temperatures are from the mid 70s to the low 90s.

Ability to Thrive in Dense Populations—Where most animals will decline if you cram too many into one small area, the German cockroach thrives and may be seen crawling over each other while still reproducing to create more.

Omnivorous—The German cockroach can feed on many types of foods; however, they do need a balanced diet to do well. Fortunately for us, once we learn their strengths and behavior patterns, we can develop a strategy to attack and destroy them. This manual will give you the knowledge that you need to succeed in your battles against the German cockroach and other types as well.

Human Behaviors *Loved* by German Cockroaches

The German cockroach has been a pest of man and his environs since before recorded history. Unfortunately, there are things humans unknowingly continue to do that serve to assure the survival of German cockroaches and even cause them to thrive within our dwellings and structures.

Timid roach, why be so shy?
We are brothers, thou and I.
In the midnight, like yourself
I explore the pantry shelf!
—Christopher Morley

CHAPTER 2: COCKROACH BIOLOGY, DEVELOPMENT, AND BEHAVIOR

Following is a list of human behaviors that assist the German cockroach to survive as pests in structures. Note that these factors may also be taken advantage of by other cockroach pest species as well.

Recycling—With the effort to be green and help the planet, we recycle various items. This recycling offers various resources for cockroaches. Soda cans and food containers with remnants of food resource provide food and harborage for cockroaches.

Garbage—In years past we used to burn garbage. Nowadays we store trash and haul it off later. Accumulations of garbage provide food, moisture, and harborage for cockroaches (see photo 2.7).

Locked Drawers—At commercial and other accounts, locked drawers, cabinets, and other storage areas prevent access for inspection and treatment.

Eating Habits—Nowadays people eat at their desk, in front of the television, in bed—virtually anywhere, spreading food debris throughout a location for cockroaches to live on.

Leave Food Out—We humans often leave food out without much thought about cockroaches. Pet food, dirty dishes, food debris, and other items present food resources that can feed roaches.

PHOTO 2.8: **Humans create garbage. Excessive trash stored within the home and overflowing dumpsters provides food and harborage resource for roaches.**

Humidifiers—Humidifiers are used during winter months to raise the humidity within the structure. Cockroaches hate dry conditions.

Hoarding—In some multifamily structures we may have people who hoard things, are not tidy, and do not keep a clean apartment. Such units become the focal point of building-wide cockroach infestations.

Pets—Some people keep multiple pets and provide food and water for these pets twenty-four hours a day.

PHOTO 2.9: **Dirty dishes and food debris left in sinks for extended period of time are a welcome mat for roaches.**

Live with Cockroaches—Some people simply *live with cockroaches* and do little, if anything, to address the infestation.

Leaks—Plumbing and other leaks provide moisture for cockroaches.

Build Poorly—Some of our structures and areas within appear to be poorly planned and provide several advantages for invading cockroaches (see photo 2.8).

PHOTO 2.10: **Poorly planned and built apartment kitchens such as this, hide water heaters in inaccessible areas such as under the countertop, which creates an ideal warm and humid environment for cockroaches.**

Basic Biology as It Pertains to Controlling Cockroaches

German cockroaches have fundamental or basic biological needs. Combine these needs with their usual behavior and the following points are useful when dealing with German cockroaches:

> - German cockroach fecal matter contains aggregation pheromones, which attract cockroaches and cause them to harbor. Look for "fecal focal points" where cockroaches accumulate.
> - German cockroaches follow along edges and other structural cues. You will often find them along moldings, columns, shelves, and other such edges.
> - Sticky traps may be used to help detect the presence and harborage areas of German cockroaches.
> - Warm, moist areas attract and harbor German cockroaches.

CHAPTER 2: COCKROACH BIOLOGY, DEVELOPMENT, AND BEHAVIOR

- Cast or shed skins, fecal droppings, and salivary material can trigger asthmatic attacks in some humans.
- Areas near open pet food containers and trash attract and harbor cockroaches.
- German cockroaches are not a "kitchen only" pest; pest professionals need to inspect all rooms.
- Egg capsules are attached to and carried by the female until ready to hatch.
- They rapidly reproduce, making early detection and complete elimination essential for success.
- Cockroaches are common pests. You have had them, have them, or will get them. Keep an eye open for them.

Chapter 3
Cockroach Identification, Inspection, and Detection

Properly identifying the pest in question is a basic fundamental of successful pest-management efforts. This is because pests have their own unique biologies, behaviors, and habits that must be considered prior to selection and implementation of your pest-management service protocol work. Even though this book is dedicated to cockroach control, there are sufficient differences in the biology, behavior, and habits of cockroach species that would necessitate correct identification of the pest roach in question.

For example, we would not be successful in controlling American cockroaches if we had misidentified them as German cockroaches or Smokey brown cockroaches. The differences in these pest cockroach species to be considered would include typical harborage locations, reproductive capacity, food preferences, and other factors.

There are many resources available to the professional pest-management industry regarding the identification of cockroaches. Pictorial keys to commonly encountered cockroach species including German, American, Australian, brown banded, Oriental, Smokey brown, and wood cockroaches are available in industry references including *Truman's Scientific Guide to Pest Management Operations*, *The Handbook of Pest Control* (Mallis), and online at the Centers for Disease Control and various university department of entomology websites as well. Refer to the resource section in the appendixes.

Perhaps the easiest way to describe the major species of cockroaches that thrive with humans is to see distinct photos in different life stages of their development. Egg capsules, nymphs (immature cockroaches), and adults look different, but it is important to be able to recognize each stage of cockroach because various stages of development are usually present at infested locations.

Along with the six most prevalent pest species—German, Brown banded, American, Oriental, Smokey brown, and Australian cockroaches—we have included a few other per-domestic cockroach species and wood cockroaches. The actual size of each species is presented in the following pages for your review.

CHAPTER 3: COCKROACH IDENTIFICATION, INSPECTION, AND DETECTION

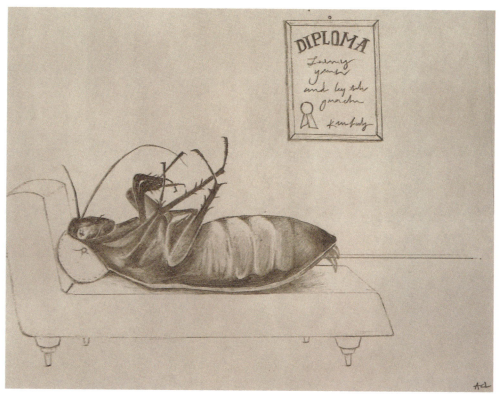

PHOTO 3.1: **It is wise to *really* get to know your pest cockroaches as well as possible.**

Profiles of Some of the Most Common Species of Cockroaches

Common Name: German Cockroach

Scientific Name: *Blatella germanica*

Nicknames: Steam fly, Croton bug (note that large numbers of these cockroaches appeared in New York shortly after the completion of the Croton Aqueduct, which supplies New York City with water. Hence a possible origin for the name; however, "croton" in Greek means tick or bug)

Size: About ½ to 5/8 inch

Color: Light brown, tan or tawny.

Markings: Two dark or black longitudinal stripes extending from the pronotum rearward on the back.

Egg capsule: About ¼ to 5/16 long, Yellowish to reddish brown in color and always carried by the female until ready to hatch.

PHOTO 3.2: **The German cockroach from egg to adult.**

Number in egg capsule: About 30 to 48. Dr. Frishman notes up to 52 individual eggs as his personal record. From four to eight capsules per lifetime.

Time to Maturity: About 36 days from hatch to reproductive adult.

Annual Descendants: As many as 400,000 from a single female.

Preferred Habitat: Cooking areas close to food and moisture sources. German cockroaches prefer warm moist areas. They aggregate near warm water pipes, under sinks, in base cabinets, stoves, hot plates, and behind refrigerators.

PHOTO 3.3: **Brown banded cockroach adult female, adult male, egg capsule, and nymph.**

Common Name: Brown Banded Cockroach

Scientific Name: *Supella longipalpa*

Nicknames: Brown bandit. (Originally introduced to the United States from Africa to Cuba in 1892 and Miami and Key West in 1903. From its humble introduction in 1903, it readily spread across the country. In 1967 it was reported in every state except Vermont. The rapid spread of this species across the United States since its introduction this century is attributable to its habit of hiding itself and its egg capsules within luggage and furniture.)

Size: About 3/8 to 1/2 inch

Color: Dark brown to pale golden.

Markings: Two transverse dark bands across the back.

Egg capsule: About ¼ to 5/16 long, Yellowish to reddish brown in color. Deposits egg capsule in out-of-the-way locations such as beneath shelves, beneath drawers, in book bindings, televisions, and other such places.

Number in Egg capsule: About 10 to 18. About ten to fourteen egg capsules per lifetime.

Time to Maturity: About 54 days from hatch to reproductive adult.

Annual Descendants: Up to 135,000 from a single female.

Preferred Habitat: Generally found in bedrooms, closets, and in piles of clothes. Prefer locations high up in heated rooms, including closet shelves, desks, bureau drawers, inside book bindings, behind frames and wallpaper, and even inside telephones and other electronics. Generally found in clusters.

CHAPTER 3: COCKROACH IDENTIFICATION, INSPECTION, AND DETECTION

Common Name: Oriental Cockroach

Scientific Name: *Blatta orientalis*

Nicknames: Water bug, black beetle, Shad roach. (In Philadelphia, its spring appearances coincides with the arrival of spawning shad fish in the Delaware River.)

Size: About 1 ¼ inch long.

Color: Nearly black in color.

Markings: Short wing stubs.

Egg capsule: Nearly black in color. Deposits egg capsules in surfaces where adults harbor including inside masonry wall voids, exterior wall, and wood surfaces.

Number in egg capsule: About 14 to 16. About eight egg capsules per lifetime.

Time to Maturity: About 128 days up to about 500 days from hatch to reproductive adult.

PHOTO 3.4: **Oriental cockroach from egg to adult.**

Annual Descendants: Up to 200 from a single female.

Preferred Habitat: Generally found in cool damp areas such as basements, crawl spaces, service ducts, and other such areas. Live in sewers and sometimes enter homes through sewage pipes or drains. Also found in toilets, bathroom sinks, and cabinets. Large numbers can congregate around various water sources.

Common Name: American Cockroach

Scientific Name: *Periplaneta americana*

Nicknames: Water bug, Palmetto bug, Bombay Canary

Size: About 1 ½ inches long.

Color: Reddish-brown to tan in color.

Markings: None other than its large size.

Egg capsule: Reddish brown to black in color. Deposits egg capsules in various places and may cover egg case in locally available debris.

Number in egg capsule: About 12 to 16. About sixty capsules per lifetime.

PHOTO 3.5: **American cockroach from egg to adult.**

Time to Maturity: About 160 days from hatch to reproductive adult.

Annual Descendants: Up to 800 from a single female.

Preferred Habitat: Generally found in damp areas such as basements, crawl spaces, service ducts, and other such areas. Live in sewers and sometimes enter homes through sewage pipes or drains. Also found in toilets, bathroom sinks, and cabinets. Frequently found in the vicinity of sewer drains.

Other Information: Develop slowly with one generation per year. Their numbers change seasonally. Most capsules are deposited in the early spring and hatch in 6 to 8 weeks. The greatest numbers of American cockroaches are observed in the summer and fall.

PHOTO 3.6: **Smokey Brown cockroach from egg to adult.**

Common Name: Smokey Brown Cockroach

Scientific Name: *Periplaneta fuliginosa*

Nicknames: Smokies.

Size: About 1 ½ inches long.

Color: Shiny brownish black to dark mahogany in color.

Markings: None other than its coloration.

Egg capsule: Reddish-brown to black in color. Deposits egg capsules in various places and may cover egg case in locally available debris.

Number in egg capsule: About 22 to 26. About seventeen egg capsules per lifetime.

Time to Maturity: From about 160 to 716 days from hatch to reproductive adult. Average is about 600 days. Can have from one to three generations per year.

Annual Descendants: Up to 200 from a single female.

Preferred Habitat: Generally found outdoors in tree holes, under logs, in leaf litter, ground cover, attics, crawl spaces, wood piles, around pet food; and debris outdoors. In sheds, garages, pump houses, and other exterior structures not frequented.

Other Information: Commonly encountered in the Southern states from the Carolinas westward to Texas. Also found in southern California, Illinois, Indiana, and Iowa. It is also common in Japan.

CHAPTER 3: COCKROACH IDENTIFICATION, INSPECTION, AND DETECTION

Common Name: Australian Cockroach

Scientific Name: *Periplaneta australasiae*

Nicknames: Pretty cockroach

Size: About 1 ¼ inches long.

Color: Reddish-brown except for a sub-marginal yellow to pale band around the edge of their pronotal shield and a pale yellow streak on the outer edge at the base of each forewing.

Markings: Pale yellow "shoulders" or area at base of forewings.

Egg capsule: Reddish brown to black in color. Deposits egg capsules in various places and may cover egg case in locally available debris.

PHOTO 3.7: **Australian cockroach adult male.**

Number in egg capsule: About 16 to 24. About twenty to thirty egg capsules per lifetime.

Time to Maturity: About one year but may range from 238 to 405 days.

Annual Descendants: Up to 200 or more from a single female.

Preferred Habitat: Do extremely well in tropical climates and rainforest areas. Populations may flourish in zoos and animal research facilities even located in northern parts of the United States. Office buildings with large indoor planters and planted areas also create a favorable habitat. Outdoors, they are confined to the warmer regions of the United States.

Other Information: Often confused for the American cockroach as their appearance is similar except for the pale-yellow shoulders and margins.

The problem with using common names for cockroaches, as well as other insects, is that these common names may mean different insects to different people, especially in different regions of the country. American cockroaches tend to be called water bugs in northern US states and Palmetto Bugs in the South. Latin names are used to exactly specify an insect species. Refer to the various photos with the Latin names included.

Why Photos May Not Be Enough

German cockroaches are distinguished by their small size and two dark, longitudinal lines extending from their pronotum toward their hind end. You might refer to them as "racing stripes." However, other species may appear to be German cockroaches and may be mistaken for them. For example, the Asian cockroach is slightly smaller and has similar coloration to the German cockroach and is often confused for the German cockroach.

Asian cockroaches can fly and are attracted to artificial lighting at night. These cockroaches feed in the landscape and may enter homes due to their attraction to light. German cockroaches cannot fly. If your customer thinks he or she has German cockroaches aggregating around the front porch light or landing on television screen at night, your customer is probably encountering the Asian cockroach. Years ago this cockroach was first encountered in Florida; however, due to its hitchhiking on vehicles, it is now found in pockets in different parts of the United States. It cannot survive in colder climates, which has prevented it becoming well established in Northern states.

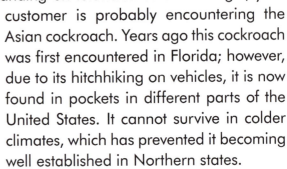

PHOTO 3.8: **Don't fall for reports of *albino* roaches. Newly molted cockroaches will appear white as is this hissing cockroach appears in the author's tank. This is commonly seen at German cockroach infested locations.**

Keep in mind that these are the six most commonly encountered pest species of cockroaches. There are plenty more species that occasionally invade, including wood, Surinam, brown, Cuban, field, Turkistan, Florida woods, Asian, and others. We are certainly not running out of cockroaches.

PHOTO 3.9: **Pennsylvannia wood cockroach.**

Chapter 4

Diseases and Damage Associated with Cockroaches

For many centuries it was thought cockroaches were just a nuisance and that disposal of some foods and objects smeared with their fecal material was not necessary. Little did we know of the large impact these creatures would have on our health and quality of our lives. We eventually learned that cockroaches were capable of contaminating foods, food preparation surfaces, and other items with various disease organisms.

Concentrating on the German cockroach, which is the most prevalent species pest professionals deal with, the primary concern associated with German cockroaches is triggering asthma attacks. The longer you live with them, the greater the probability that an attack will occur. Speaking to a family court judge in Brooklyn, New York, in the late 1990s, Dr. Frishman was surprised to learn that the primary reason young children missed school was because of asthma attacks.

How can cockroaches be blamed for this? It turns out that during the molting process, small pieces of the cast skin are produced. These tiny pieces are small and light enough that they may become airborne. Asthmatic reactions may be triggered in susceptible children and others who inhale these cast-off skin pieces. Cockroach feces and salivary secretions are also problematic. To substantiate the judges' remark, in 1998 Dr. Frishman was invited to speak at the Albert Einstein College of Medicine. All the other speakers were medical doctors. Dr. Frishman's role was to inform the medical doctor attendees about what to communicate to parents of children with asthma.

Of significance was that the medical profession was admitting they could not solve the asthma problem with medication. It was an environmental situation that could only be corrected by the elimination of the source of the allergens, which was the cockroaches.

During the mid 1990s Paul Bello was based in metro Atlanta, working as a technical representative with Zeneca Professional Products. At that time a story ran in an Atlanta newspaper about an eight-month-old infant girl who choked to death after the inadvertent aspiration of a live (German) cockroach.

Clearly the work we do as pest-management professionals is important for many reasons, including the health and welfare of our customers. We have to eliminate the cockroaches.

Dr. David L. Rosenstreich, MD, et al., published a paper in the *New England Journal of Medicine* (Vol. 336, 356–1363 [May 8 1997]). In this paper it was concluded that "the combination of cockroach allergy and exposure to high levels of this allergen may help explain the frequency of asthma related health problems in inner city children." Because the information presented in this paper is so important to a better understanding of why humans *must* not live with cockroaches, the abstract of this paper is presented below:

Abstract

Background: It has been hypothesized that asthma-related problems are most severe among children in inner-city areas who are allergic to a specific allergen and also exposed to high levels of that allergen in bedroom dust.

Methods: From November 1992 through October 1993, we recruited 476 children with asthma (age four to nine years) from eight inner-city areas in the United States. Immediate hypersensitivity to cockroach, house dust mite, and cat allergens were measured by skin testing. When we measured major allergens of cockroach (Bla 1), dust mites (Der p 1 and Der f 1), and cat dander (Fel d 1) in household dust using monoclonal-antibody-based enzyme-linked immunosorbent assays. High levels of exposure were defined according to proposed thresholds for causing disease. Data on morbidity due to asthma were collected at base line and over a one year period.

Results: Of the children, 36.8 percent were allergic to cockroach allergen, 34.9 percent to dust mite, and 22.7 percent to cat allergen. Among the children's bedrooms, 50.2 percent had high levels of cockroach allergen in dust, 9.7 percent had high levels of dust mite allergen and 12.6 percent had high levels of cat allergen. After we adjusted for sex, score on the Child Behavior Checklist and family history of asthma, we found that children who were both allergic to cockroach allergen and exposed to high levels of this allergen had 0.37 hospitalization a year, as compared with 0.11 for the other children (P=0.001), and 2.56 unscheduled medical visits for asthma per year, as compared with 1.43 (P< 0.001). They also had significantly more days of wheezing, missed school days, and nights with lost sleep and their parents or other care givers were awakened during the night and changed their daytime plans because of the child's asthma significantly more frequently. Similar patterns were not found for the combination of allergy to dust mites or cat dander and high levels of the allergen.

Conclusions: The combination of cockroach allergy and exposure to high levels of this allergen may help explain the frequency of asthma related health problems in inner-city children. (*New England Journal of Medicine* 1997, Vol 336, 1356–63).

Interestingly enough, mice and house dust mites ranked second and third for causes of asthmatic reactions. All underscore the importance and need for proper pest management.

In developing countries where dwellings are not so airtight, the incidence of asthma is less. In Georgia there was a case where an apartment was treated for cockroaches and the

CHAPTER 4: DISEASES AND DAMAGE ASSOCIATED WITH COCKROACHES

tenant died when he returned after the treatment. At first most suspected it was caused by pesticide exposure, but this was not the case. The cockroach treatment work, and perhaps the pesticide(s) used, flushed the cockroaches and kicked up allergenic material, thus increasing the exposure to the tenant. He was a person known to previously have had a severe reaction to cockroaches. Because of this awareness, I (Dr. A. M. Frishman) was motivated to write an article for *Pest Management Professional* magazine on how a pest professional should avoid such a disaster. (See Appendix 1 for details.)

Keep in mind that even when we totally eliminate the cockroaches from a customer's home, the allergen materials remains. Different studies have shown that it is extremely difficult if not impossible to remove all these allergen materials. The stability of the cockroach allergens (called Bla g1 and Bla g2) is unfortunately persistent. Studies show that nine months after all the cockroaches in an infested household have been eliminated, the allergen levels remain sufficiently high enough to continue to generate allergenic symptoms.

"While people have always known that cockroach allergy is an important causal agent, the magnitude of it wasn't appreciated until now."—Robert B. Mellind, President, American Lung Association of NY, 1997.

The good news is that once the live cockroaches have been eliminated, it is enough to significantly reduce recurring asthma attacks.

In 1980, Dr. I. Edward Alcamo and Dr. Austin M. Frishman published a paper in the *Journal of Environmental Health* verifying that domestic cockroaches collected in different types of structures carry various detrimental bacteria. Summary tables from that publication appear here, and the complete publication is in the appendix.

Comon Infections Associated With Bacteria Sought		
Type	**Infection**	**Comments**
Staphyloccus	Intestinal food poisoning. Skin boils and carbuncles staph infection.	Produces a toxin which irritates the intestinal lining. The most common source of food poisoining in the U.S.
Streptococcus	Intenstinal food poisoning.	Used as an indicator of fecal contamination of waters.
Coliform bacteria	Various human infections including gastroenteritis, rinary tract infections, diarrhea, blood and wound infections.	Used as a general indicator of fecal contamination of waters. Includes Escherichia, Klebsiella, Enterobacter, Serraria and others.
Eshcerichia Coli	Epidemic diarrhea of infants, urinary tract infection, nephritis.	U.S. waters.Used as a specific indicator of fecal contamination of
Salmonella	Typhoid fever, Salmonellosis, intestinal food infection.	Diseases range from extremely serious to milder intestinal disorders. Commonly found in the human intestine and in contaminated food.
Shigella	Bacterial dysentery.	Serious intenstinal disease with sever dehydration. Spread by human carriers.

PHOTO 4.1: **This chart lists the bacteria pathogens tested for in the field study conducted by Drs. Frishman and Alcamo.**

Food Poisoning Bacteria Found in Field Collected Cockroaches		
Pathogen	Number of Locations	Infestation Level
Coliform	84%	High
Eshcerichia Coli	24%	High
Salmonella	4%	Low
Shigella	0%	NA
Staphylococcus	76%	High
Streptococcus	8%	High

PHOTO 4.2: **Results of bacteria found on wild-caught cockroaches.**

Of concern is the occurrence of MRSA (Methicillin-resistant *Staphylococcus aureus*, a bacterium responsible for several difficult-to-treat infections in humans) becoming an increasingly major problem in health-care facilities. Since we already know cockroaches can mechanically transmit disease pathogens, the potential exists for them to carry and spread MRSA to humans and pets with open wounds. This concern is based on experience and review of previous publications.

In reviewing a very practical research project, Jacqueline Ferguson, a nursing student at a university hospital selected an interesting project for her masters thesis: "Can and would German cockroaches penetrate double-wrapped and steam autoclaved sterile packs prepared for surgery?" If so, would they contaminate the utensils inside with pathogenic bacteria? Both events proved true. This resulted in an immediate change in how the hospital stored the sterile surgery packs. Interestingly enough, the nursing student's husband was a pest-management professional at the time.

Aside from the medical importance associated with pathogenic bacteria, cockroaches cause physical abuse to humans. Sad and incredible as it may seem, children and adults at infested locations have had their eyelashes removed by cockroaches while they slept. Finger and toenails are also chewed on. Open wounds may be fed upon and sores may be manifested upon a person's body by cockroaches, all while sleeping. For this to occur, the cockroach density has to be very high, but this does occur and has been reported by pest professionals in a number of locations while also being observed by the authors of this book.

While servicing an account in Monticello, New York, I (Dr. Frishman) came across it for the first time—two children had no eyelashes, and the mother calmly told me the cockroaches had eaten them. When I finished treating, it "rained" cockroaches enough that I could sweep up a pile in just one room. Then I believed her. To top it off, at first the woman refused to let me in to treat! That was my first experience in understanding just how important cockroach elimination is. I encountered it several times since over the years. It is not uncommon for pest-management service technicians to exchange real-life war stories on how bad a cockroach job that had to be tackled was. Another reason we call this book *The Cockroach Combat Manual II*.

CHAPTER 4: DISEASES AND DAMAGE ASSOCIATED WITH COCKROACHES

Besides their ability to contaminate foods, food-preparation surfaces, and spread diseases, cockroaches can also cause damage. These insects can destroy electrical appliances, smoke detectors, clothing, and photos just by their numbers. When present in large numbers and over long periods of time, they can damage various items by depositing their fecal smears that stick to surfaces where they harbor. Fecal smears can contaminate and foul electronics, utensils, medical equipment, and many other objects.

Perhaps the saddest realization is that the poorer the affected people are, the more they may have to discard due to cockroach contamination, and the more they may have to spend on do-it-yourself control products that many of these people can ill afford. Cockroaches have been found naturally contaminated with about forty different species of bacteria that are detrimental to vertebrates. These do not include the additional bacteria that cockroaches can easily pick up on the exterior of their exoskeleton as they move throughout an infested location.

Chapter 5

Cockroach Inspection and Detection

Cockroach Inspections

Pest-management references have long presented the critical role a thorough inspection plays in the success of pest-management programs. No program can be successful without sound inspection procedures. Inspections are critical in determining the extent of the pest problem, the reasons for the pest problem, and for discovering the various corrective actions that may be implemented for the long-term successful control of the pest problem.

PHOTO 5.1: **Whether bed bugs or cockroaches, a thorough inspection is critical to the success of your treatment and elimination work.**

It would be difficult at best to conduct a suitable inspection for cockroaches without proper equipment with which to conduct the inspection. "When I go hunting for cockroaches, I go loaded for bear. My tools are essential to making the hunt successful," says Dr. Frishman, who has presented these concepts to pest-management technicians attending his presentations for decades. Over the years, experienced professionals have learned that being properly equipped can significantly enhance the inspection process.

CHAPTER 5: COCKROACH INSPECTION AND DETECTION

PHOTO 5.2: **Removal of drawers and a good flashlight are fundamentals of a thorough cockroach inspection.**

While each of us may have our favorite individual pieces of inspection equipment, the following list includes various items that may be used to conduct superior inspections along with some comments for your review.

> **Knee Pads**—The areas we inspect vary in their degree of cleanliness, texture, infestation, and other local conditions. Using knee pads serves to protect our knees from hard surfaces, sharp objects, and in some cases wet areas. While Dr. Frishman points out that using knee pads has allowed him to save his knees over the seventy-three years of his life, there is no doubt that using professional-style knee pads during inspections is beneficial. Note that knee pads come in many styles and costs. However, those models with hinged articulating joints that have the ability to bend along with the wearer's knee tend to remain in place and simply work better than non-articulating models.

> **Flashlights**—Clearly we pest-management professionals are constantly seeking the best flashlights we can possibly find. With the recent widespread availability of LED-style flashlights, the industry has benefited from superior flashlights to those from years ago and have reduced costs as the availability of this technology grows. It is wise to carry two flashlights so you have a backup, while also carrying extra batteries if needed. As the race for more lumens progresses, some technicians may find their LED flashlight too bright for inspection purposes. However, some flashlights may offer high- and low-beam settings, which may adequately address this concern. It is also wise to use an LED-style headlight, as doing so provides the professional light and the ability to work hands-free.

➤ **Sticky traps**—Cockroaches may be monitored and detected through the use of sticky traps. Remember that sticky traps work for us 24/7 and provide tangible evidence that may be used for various reasons when dealing with an infested location. Refer to "12 Ways to Read a Sticky Trap" and related articles in Appendix I.

PHOTO 5.3: **Sticky traps work 24/7 for the pest professional and help detect cockroaches as well as identify areas of infestation.**

➤ **Gloves**—When working with cockroaches and within cockroach environs, we may be subjected to a variety of pathogens. At certain accounts we will encounter surfaces fouled with grease, food debris, bacteria, and other undesirable substances that we may not wish to touch with our bare hands. While some professionals choose disposable gloves, others may opt for more robust, chemically resistant types.

➤ **Hand tools**—No matter what type of pest management work is being done, hand tools are necessary. Screwdrivers, pliers, and wrenches may be needed to open certain areas of equipment, open access panels, or remove coverings. It may be necessary to open areas for inspection and/or treatment purposes to hidden areas where cockroaches may harbor. Drills may be needed to create ports through which insecticide products, such as dusts, may be applied. Multi-tool devices such as the Leatherman and similar tools provide the convenience of versatility because such tools include a blade, pliers, cutting pliers, file, screwdriver, and other options. Pry bars and jacks may be used to lift heavy objects for service and inspections.

➤ **Inspection mirror**—Inspection mirrors are available in various models. We prefer mirrors that are made of metal and not those with glass as the reflective surface. Inspection mirrors may be used to inspect areas that are not easily seen with the naked eye. Inspection mirrors are a useful tool that allow us to see behind and beneath objects when checking for the presence of cockroaches and other pests.

CHAPTER 5: COCKROACH INSPECTION AND DETECTION

PHOTO 5.4: **Use of an inspection mirror allows visual access to difficult to reach areas and saves time. Also note use of knee pads by this technician.**

> **Digital camera**—Nowadays nearly every cell phone contains a digital camera. The price of a suitable digital camera is very much affordable. Such cameras may also be used to shoot video clips. Photos taken may be used to document your inspection as well as to inform the client of certain conducive conditions that need correction. Additionally, such photos may be used for technician training. Note that in commercial accounts permission must be attained prior to taking photos.

> **Hand duster**—An empty hand duster may be used to squeeze small puffs of air, which can flush cockroaches hidden deep within cracks and crevices that might not otherwise come out. Note that flushing with an insecticide product may cause too many cockroaches to flush, presenting the inspector and the customer with an additional problem. An aerosol air can may be used in a similar fashion.

> **Step ladder**—A ladder is absolutely necessary when access to overhead and out-of-reach areas is required for inspection and treatment work. Be sure technicians are suitably trained to use a ladder safely.

> **Borescope Camera**—Such digital cameras are now available from various sources. These cameras may be inserted into confined areas that may be too small to physically enter ourselves and allow for video viewing of such areas. However, when insulation and other items are present within the areas being inspected, the view through such borescopes may be limited.

Cockroach Inspections: Where to Look

When hunting for cockroaches, it's best to know in advance their tendencies and preferences. This way, you'll shorten your search and become more time-efficient in your work. Each species may have its own preferences and tendencies. When searching for cockroaches, we need to have the proper mindset.

PHOTO 5.5: **Look carefully for antenna protruding from cockroach harborages such as floor drains and other areas where roaches hide.**

"You have to think like a roach," Dr. Frishman says, and he's right. Yes, many of us have heard Doc tell us that for years, but it's a fundamental that can't be overlooked in cockroach work. And what's meant by this is to know the cockroach's preferences and look where you'd hide if you were a cockroach. So, as Dr. Frishman tells us, "Think like a roach, and you will be drawn to where they hide."

CHAPTER 5: COCKROACH INSPECTION AND DETECTION

PHOTO 5.6: **Open ranges and remove kick plates from dishwashers and refrigerators to inspect and treat for hidden cockroaches.**

Remember that cockroaches fundamentally prefer warm, moist areas where cracks and crevices are present. You may need to crawl on your belly, slide on your back, or even crawl into a cabinet to be able to access all hidden areas and conduct a thorough cockroach inspection. The following are the top locations where cockroaches harbor or hide:

- Wet areas near sinks, faucets, over-watered plants, pet water bowls, condensation pans under refrigerators, floor drains, cracks in floors that hold water, and other such places
- Warm areas near motors, radiators, ovens, stoves, and up high at ceiling moldings
- Water heaters often hidden from view and inaccessible in apartments and other small living locations
- Difficult to reach and undisturbed areas such as behind a refrigerator or freezer. Such areas may be located high or low.
- Boxes piled up against walls
- Cardboard and paper materials not moved for extended periods of time
- Locked areas normally not accessible for inspection including the liquor storage room in commercial accounts, drawers, closets, and other such areas. While it may be locked to humans, it's not inaccessible to cockroaches and other pests.
- Areas where cockroach fecal stains are present.
- Look for waving antenna (that looks like thin hair) protruding from cracks and crevices where the cockroaches are hiding.
- Cockroaches also prefer to hide along structural edges. Inspect edges and corners of shelves, moldings, bulletin boards, and other such places.
- Pet bowls may attract cockroaches.

Even though we diligently inspect these areas, we may not find cockroaches in every place we look. This is why it's important to remain persistent during your inspection, to keep searching and be thorough. The best cockroach inspectors keep looking and don't stop until they've found cockroach harborages.

Practical Cockroach Inspection Tips

The following practical inspection tips are provided for the benefit of the reader for use during upcoming cockroach inspections. This list is targeted to pest-control professionals.

1. Inspecting for cockroaches can be dirty work. Be properly prepared.
2. Bring a suitable change of clothes in the event you get too dirty to enter your own vehicle or the next customer's location.
3. Use gloves and suitable work clothes when inspecting for cockroaches.
4. An LED-type headlight can provide hands-free lighting in dark places when inspecting for cockroaches.
5. Always have backup batteries on hand during your inspection and treatment work.
6. Use a hard hat or bump cap to protect your head from injury during your inspections.

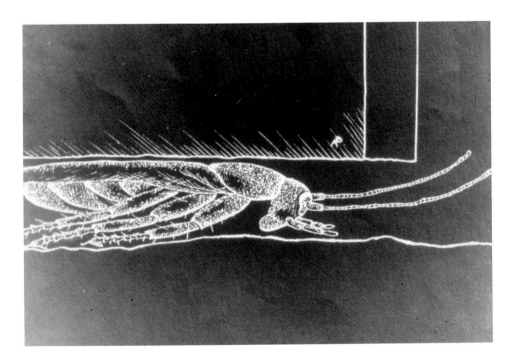

PHOTO 5.7: **Cockroaches are thigmotropic which means they prefer to hide in tight places such that their tarsi and dorsal side are in contact with surfaces as pictured here.**

7. Cockroaches may be hiding in a table or other similarly sized item. Lift a table slightly and drop it quickly. When it hits the floor, if cockroaches are there, they'll fall off.
8. Well placed sticky-trap monitors help pinpoint cockroach harborage locations.
9. Pull items away from walls to expose otherwise difficult-to-reach areas.

CHAPTER 5: COCKROACH INSPECTION AND DETECTION

10. Be sure to speak to the person who arrives first in the morning to turn on the lights; he or she knows where the roaches are and run to when the lights come on.
11. People tend to tell us that they see cockroaches "all over." Ask politely *where* they see them, *when* they see them, and *the last place* they saw them.
12. Work in a 3D or multilevel fashion. Work floor level, midlevel, and high-level inspection.
13. Use a hand duster to puff air into suspect void areas to flush roaches.
14. Be considerate of the account you're handling when inspecting for cockroaches. A food-service manager doesn't want you flushing cockroaches at inopportune times during the hours of operation.
15. You need access and visibility to successfully inspect for roaches and other pests.
16. When inspecting a kitchen, be sure to remove cabinet drawers and inspect the areas within the cabinetry where roaches will harbor and deposit their fecal matter.
17. Use an inspection mirror to enhance your inspection. These mirrors may be used to see hidden areas above, below, and behind areas you normally may not be able to see without the mirror. Inspection mirrors are available from tool, equipment, and other suppliers.
18. A chrome-type inspection mirror, the type where the reflective surface is metal, is more durable then a glass-type inspection mirror.
19. A mechanical reaching and clasping device may be useful during the inspection process to retrieve and subsequently replace sticky traps.
20. An aerosol air cleaner may also be used for gentle and discrete flushing of roaches.
21. Dig deeper when you find something and do so in a 3D-spherical fashion around the original sighting area.

PHOTO 5.8: **Sticky traps work 24/7 and help the technician to find areas of roach activity that may go unnoticed.**

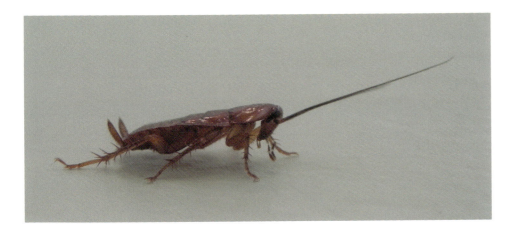

PHOTO 5.9: **Cockroach bodies are built rather flat allowing them it enter and hide via amazingly small cracks, crevices and holes.**

22. Place additional sticky traps in an area where you find even one cockroach.
23. If a room is dark when you enter, leave the lights off and search with just your flashlight to see what you can find. You may be surprised to see many cockroaches doing what cockroaches normally do when the lights are out. Then turn the lights on and watch where the roaches run.
24. Be sure to get an LED-type flashlight; they're brighter, the batteries last much longer when compared to regular type lights, and they are available at reasonable prices.
25. Access to hidden areas where roaches may harbor, breed, and build populations is required during your inspection. Such locations serve to cause ongoing sightings at infested locations. Be sure to communicate this to your customer when accessibility becomes an issue barring your complete inspection of a location.

Chapter 6

Cockroach Trivia and Records, Unusual Circumstances, and Worst-Case Scenarios

All cockroaches can swim for short periods. Of the domestic species, Oriental and American cockroaches are the best swimmers. They are often associated with sewers and can swim through pipes. Some non-domestic cockroaches live in and near water, while others are desert dwellers.

Some species can hiss or whistle by forcing air through their spiracles (small breathing ports on the sides of their bodies). The loudest are the *Gromphadorhina* spp. They are sometimes called hissing cockroaches. They hiss when disturbed, when people pick them up, and for other reasons. The sound of the hissing mimics that of a snake and may be a defense mechanism.

Blaberus giganteus, a tropical species, is the largest cockroach species in the world. These cockroaches are kept by entomologists in rearing containers primarily as conversation pieces. These cockroaches live under rocks and in caves in Panama and palm trees in Trinidad. They measure approximately three inches in length, not counting their long antennae.

PHOTO 6.1: **Madagascar hissing cockroaches force air through their spiracles to make a hissing noise. Pest professionals keep these roaches for conducting bug classes at schools and other purposes. Note the recently molted albino roach.**

The American cockroach holds the record for the longest distance traveled through sewers that was scientifically recorded. One has been documented as having traveled a total of 385 yards, nearly the length of four football fields. This record was authenticated by capturing live cockroaches in a sewer followed by tagging each cockroach as one might tag a bird and then releasing them back into the sewer system at the same point where they were captured. This work was conducted in Tyler, Texas.

It is not uncommon to find American cockroaches clinging to the upper surfaces of sewer pipes upside down. Normally such sewer pipes are not completely full, which provides much inner pipe surface upon which the cockroaches can cling, travel, and forage. In heavy rains these pipes may flood, and the cockroaches migrate in large numbers to nearby basements to avoid drowning. They can detect changes in barometric pressures and may know when to take to the high ground. In Bermuda, thousands of cockroaches have been observed running across the highway about an hour prior to a heavy downpour. Native Bermudians recognize this as a signal of forthcoming rain.

Cockroaches can hide or scurry into the smallest places imaginable. A newborn cockroach can hide in a crack or crevice just one half of a millimeter wide, which is about as thin as a sheet of paper. A hungry adult male German cockroach can fit through a crack thinner than a dime.

The Velsicol Chemical Company developed a fictitious character named "Rudy the Roach" as part of a national sales campaign. The company marketed T-shirts and buttons emblazoned with their character.

A few toy companies have experimented with rubber cockroaches.

Max Force's Gordon Morrison, currently with Bayer Environmental Science, had flip flops made with the likeness of cockroach cutouts imprinted on the soles. As wearers walked along the beach, a cockroach was imprinted on the sand in each footprint.

PHOTO 6.2: **This sticky trap was full after just overnight placement at an infested apartment underscoring that German cockroaches can build large populations in short periods.**

Some pest-control companies adorn their service vehicles with huge pests, including large, four-foot-long model cockroaches.

A story circulated amongst pest control professionals depicts a woman in Miami, Florida, who was seen in a supermarket leading a large cockroach on a leash. To date this story has never been substantiated.

Some pest-control technicians have been assaulted or harassed by apartment dwellers who have developed a personal liking for their "pet" cockroaches and have feared they might be exterminated. Pet cockroaches are inadvisable because of their ability to carry and transmit disease.

In 1965, in Lafayette, Indiana, more than six thousand German cockroaches were found in a single case of beer.

On August 1, 1947, a four-room apartment in Austin, Texas, was treated for German cockroaches. Approximately one hundred thousand German cockroaches were killed that day.

In 1967, when Stanley Rachesky, an entomologist and author, tested the effects of the insecticide Baygon, he collected more than 132 pounds of dead American cockroaches from the cage of Sinbad the Gorilla at the Lincoln Park Zoo in Chicago.

At an average weight of about 30 g or 1.1 ounces, each there are fewer than twenty adult American cockroaches per pound.

At an average weight of about 0.1 to 0.12 g each, there are approximately 4,540 adult German cockroaches per pound.

In the 1880s, according to army records unearthed by Smithsonian Institute researchers, a brigade of men wielding brooms were unable to halt a mass migration of cockroaches out of a Washington DC restaurant and into the United States Capitol building. Today, "We can't seem to get rid of them," stated a despairing official in the Capitol architect's office.

In 1977 three New York University students made the news when they bought a foot-long gecko lizard to eat the cockroaches in their Greenwich Village apartment. "We had so many cockroaches the kitchen sink was black at night," complained one student. After several months, the lizard began to get the upper hand in control of the problem. "We used to hear him crunching on them at night. It woke us up at first, but after a few nights we got used to it," another student added. The story appeared in the *New York Times*.

In May 1938 a prisoner in the Amarillo, Texas, jail told how he trained a cockroach to come to his solitary confinement cell when he whistled. The cockroach would come with a cigarette tied to its back.

Cockroaches are closely related to termites. In Australia there is a termite that deposits eggs in a capsule similar to the one produced by some cockroach species.

In 1969 in Woodbridge Township, New Jersey, it was reported that hordes of cockroaches invaded homes during the night in search of food. "It's like something in the movies," said a distressed homeowner whose house was one of ten severely overrun by the insects. "Armies of them march across the street every night," she said.

Peter C. Sheretz, a professor at Virginia Commonwealth University in Richmond, says the hardy cockroach can dine on lethal cancer-causing toxins without any harmful effects. He expressed the hope that this finding may be helpful in discovering a cure for cancer. "I fed them higher concentrations of the cancer-causing agent than a lot of other researchers have fed to other animals that got cancer. They ate until they really died of old age," Sheretz said.

On December 13, 1976, the *Long Island Press* reported Bruce Hammock, an insect endocrinologist, kept five hundred giant Madagascar and Panamanian cockroaches locked in a special escape-proof lab at the University of California at Riverside. "These are the biggest cockroaches on Earth," Hammock stated, fondling the cockroaches and allowing them to crawl on his lab coat. He was working on finding a synthetic hormone that can replace insecticides.

Women entomologists have been at the forefront in research on cockroaches. At the American Museum of Natural History in New York City, Dr. Betty Lane Faber, now retired, had been tagging cockroaches and studying their behavior. She reported that "male cockroaches stay out later than female ones and that all roaches give off a distinctive scented signal—a pheromone—that attracts other roaches." She observed that although cockroaches may not have a clear sense of territoriality, they do appear to stay in one place most of their lives. Since most of their activity is at night, Dr. Faber often slept on a cot in her laboratory and woke to track her tagged cockroaches with a flashlight and camera. Dr. Faber's observations were reported in the *New York Times*.

Another noted female researcher was Alice Gray, an insect specialist at the American Museum of Natural History. She is well remembered for sponsoring the first public cockroach exhibition at the museum called "Roaches Are Here to Stay" in 1973. She had been remarkable in helping thousands of students become interested in insects and entomology. She believed cockroaches should be admired for their beauty and ability to adapt.

Dr. Ruth Simon, a member of the US Geological Survey, observed that cockroaches can predict earthquakes. "Before an earthquake of small intensity, there's a marked increase in activity," she reports.

Research conducted in 1977 by Genie Floyd, a freshman at New College, Sarasota, Florida, indicates that cold cockroaches are smarter than warm ones. This marine biology major found that cockroaches that had been subjected to temperature of forty-three degrees F made fewer errors when escaping from a maze than did cockroaches kept at seventy-three degrees F.

Dr. F. A. McKittrick is another noted female entomologist who specialized in the study of the evolution of cockroaches and has published significant work on this topic.

CHAPTER 6: COCKROACH TRIVIA AND RECORDS, UNUSUAL CIRCUMSTANCES, AND WORST-CASE SCENARIOS

Women have also been entering the field of professional pest management. In New York City, two women founded a company named Lady Bug Pest Control, and another woman called her business The Elegant Exterminator.

Cockroaches have been known to foul electronics and prevent them from properly working. Cockroaches have chewing mouthparts with tooth-like mandibles that are capable of destroying wires and circuit boards. Their fecal matter may also foul electronic circuitry. Appliances, radios, computers, telephones, and other electronic devices may be ruined by cockroaches.

Dr. Frishman encountered an extremely heavy population living inside a console-type radio at a large city hospital. There were so many cockroaches that it was difficult to read the printed radio station markings. The cockroaches were clustered just behind the plastic protecting the dial. Thousands more were hidden behind the back plate. In order to survive, the cockroaches would rush out at night and drink urine off the floor, which had been spilled by patients who could not control themselves. Dr. Frishman had been called in to advise on this situation. His solution was simple. He placed a large plastic bag over the entire console and placed a pyrethrin bomb inside to destroy the population. A few hours later he vacuumed up the dead cockroaches and restored the console for the entertainment of the patients.

The callitrichid monkey removes the head, guts, wings, and legs off a cockroach prior to eating it.

Cockroaches are found throughout the world. In 1977, the *New York Times* reported that among the products most sought after by the diplomatic community in Moscow was cockroach spray.

PHOTO 6.3: **Large populations of German cockroach infestations continue to occur as indicated by this toilet full of roaches.** Photo courtesy of George Williams, BCE of EHS.

According to Alice Gray of the American Museum of Natural History, few cultures accord the cockroach any reverence. Only in India and Polynesia can jewelry and ornaments devoted to the cockroach be found.

On November 20, 1978, the *New York Times* reported that despite pesticide bombing of forty-five hundred Metropolitan Transit Authority buses every other weekend, this effort had failed to control cockroaches living in the seats, walls, and floors of the buses.

During the late 1990s, Paul Bello was called to provide advice on the infestation present within the *Biosphere* located in the Arizona desert. The facility was to be renovated and configured for other purposes; however, there were many species not indigenous to the Arizona desert that authorities did not want to inadvertently introduce. Amongst the insect pests present were a number of cockroaches, including exotic species. Species included American cockroaches, which were purposefully there, Surinam cockroaches, lobster cockroaches, and Turkistan cockroaches.

Cockroaches have been implicated in the mechanical transmission of certain disease pathogens including MRSA.

In 2012, when visiting the New York Public Library for purposes of donating copies of *The Bed Bug Combat Manual,* one librarian reported that each summer her condominium complex located in Huntington, New York, becomes inundated with thousands of Oriental cockroaches. "There are thousands of them all over the walkways and climbing up on the screen door every night," she said. Checking with local pest professionals in the area confirmed that in the past few years, Oriental cockroaches have become a significant recurring problem.

Recently Dr. Frishman visited and advised on two public high schools located on Long Island that were inundated with Oriental cockroaches. At night the cockroaches were crawling on the lawn, the walkways, and up the exterior walls. "We found them hiding in the drop ceiling, the masonry wall voids, and in steam tunnels," he reported. Glue boards placed in such locations are full in fewer than twenty-four hours. Reportedly, this has been occurring during the spring and summer months since around the year 2000.

Worst-Case Scenarios

The primary purpose of relating to these stories is not for the sensation factor. It is to stress to PMPs what might happen if our profession did not exist. It emphasizes how horrible a cockroach situation can become and the incredible horror humans must, or mistakenly think they must, endure on a daily and nightly basis in their own homes. It shows that humans can give up on themselves and suffer beyond what you would believe humanly possible. The victims are often children, the elderly, and the poor. It underscores how important our work can be to others who depend on us.

With today's technology, there is no excuse. It is not a shame to have cockroaches. It is a shame to persist with them. Never let this happen in your own accounts. Do what you can to correct it wherever it exists. Do your best.

Built small, so they are able to hide in many places, with keen senses that help them detect danger as well as much needed resources, and having the ability to reproduce at a rapid rate all contribute to the success of German cockroaches as a pest species. The American cockroach, a much larger species, is also a successful pest species but may be due to different advantage factors.

American cockroaches are faster, capable of ranging great distances for various resources, and may harbor in difficult-to-access locations far from where we might expect at an account. These factors and others allow these cockroaches to build significant populations at infested account locations, which make for worst-case scenarios.

For the majority of people who live in private homes, the thought of having to live with cockroaches on a permanent basis is incomprehensible. For apartment dwellers and folks who live in certain locations, this is not always the case. The events you are about to review are true. We witnessed them and share them with you for your benefit.

Horror Stories: American Cockroaches

Austin M. Frishman, PhD

I have no problem recalling the most horrendous cockroach job I ever tackled. It is the only one that literally gave me nightmares, where I would wake up in the middle of the night sweating. It was an American cockroach job in a hospital on Long Island, New York.

At this location I was testing a new gel cockroach bait that needed a tough test. Under an entire hospital was a crawl space about two-and-a-half-feet high containing many steam pipes and other obstacles. When you dropped down through the floor via a hatchway, it was teeming with well more than three hundred thousand cockroaches. There were so many they were hanging vertically on each other's backs, covering the vertical pillars.

There was a sewerage leak that was decades old. The cockroaches were feeding on the crusted fecal material. When you lifted the crusted material, hundreds to thousands of young nymphs scurried about. A few cockroaches were feeding on dead rats. As I put the gel baits out, the cockroaches came running to the bait, devouring it. They were fighting each other to get to the bait, many of them trying to crawl up on me while crouched in this area that one could truly describe as the cesspool of life.

I had to return to this location and bait six more times. At no time could I ever get someone to return with me a second time. The gel became registered as MAXFORCE Gel Cockroach Bait.

Sanitary landfills can create a cockroach haven. Unfortunately, sometimes public housing is built over such old abandoned sites. In such situations, American cockroaches will continue to emerge into homes for the next one hundred years or more.

My first encounter was in a snowstorm in Waltham, Massachusetts. I was training technicians how to use a rodent bait on the landfill. There was about six inches of snow on the ground and snowing heavily. As we raked back snow and debris from the surface of the landfill, American cockroaches came bubbling out onto the surface. *No way,* I thought. Here is a tropical insect surviving in a northern state outdoors in the winter, on the snow! The heat from the fermenting garbage provided them with enough warmth to survive and thrive.

To control these insects, you would have to set up *drums* of cockroach bait (like NIBAN Granular) and let it flow into feeding stations placed around the perimeter and in the landfill. A few hundred pounds of bait would not be excessive to handle a heavy cockroach population such as this. They might eat that much in a few days. You would have to refill the drums for continued baiting.

For years, animal research facilities battle unchecked German and American cockroach populations because no pesticides could be used around the research animals. The cockroaches would physically abuse the animals by chewing on their hair and body. This, of course, put the test animals under stress, which affected and invalidated the research results. I would watch animal lab technicians attempt to use flamethrowers to fry the cockroaches when the animals were temporarily removed. They used steam, high water pressure, and just physically crushing them all to no satisfactory conclusion.

One of the most difficult cockroach jobs I ever encountered looked relatively simple to start with. It involved a greenhouse with plants for teaching purposes and a few research monkeys. American cockroaches were destroying the plants and harassing the monkeys. No residual baits or sprays were permitted. We were permitted to space treat with a pyrethrin (organic) base product.

We started about eight p.m. The monkeys were removed for treatment. The greenhouse was closed up and the space treated. Every hour it was retreated until six o'clock the next morning. That was eleven treatments. It was aerated and the monkeys brought back in. Within two days, American cockroaches resurfaced. A further investigation showed they were living in rat burrows hidden below workbenches. We had to fill in every rat burrow and redo the entire job.

Years later, during daytime hours, while dusting rat burrows around trees on Park Avenue in NYC, we unknowingly flushed American cockroaches onto the sidewalk. Only in NYC do people walk by and keep on walking unfazed as the cockroaches scooted between their legs to avoid getting trampled. We had to stand guard by one store to head off a few frantic cockroaches headed indoors. We did a *Mexican hat dance* to stop the ones running amuck. This without the advantage of wearing pointed shoes.

German Cockroaches—Horror Stories

Paul J. Bello

Working as a pest management technician supported and provided me a dimension of training that could not be attained in the classroom. One day I was assigned to conduct a cockroach cleanout at a Section 8-type apartment complex. It was a one-bedroom occupied by a mom and her toddler son. Visible signs and odors of German cockroaches was readily apparent in every room, and as a young technician, some of the thoughts that ran through my mind included but were not limited to, *This is just like we learned about in Dr. Frishman's class. How can people live like this?*, and *Wow, one look at the boy's face tells me these cockroaches are so bad here that he's missing eyelashes and eyebrows.*

One look in the kitchen sink base cabinet showed that this apartment had what we learned to term "3-D roaches." Three-dimensional cockroaches is when there are so many that there is limited cabinet wall space—cockroaches are hanging off cockroaches. In any case, there were a lot of cockroaches in this apartment, such that what was in the cabinets looked much like what we had seen in one of Dr. Frishman's lab rearing jars. There were countless thousands in this apartment.

Back in the day and looking back to those times, it seemed that we just didn't know all that we needed to know. Clearly, the school of hard knocks is a great teacher, where oftentimes lessons are learned in such a way that we just don't forget. Our tools of choice at that time were dominated by water-mixed liquid concentrates as well as aerosol spray-type products. We also used oil-based products, applied via various ultra-low or ULV-type injection, as well as aerosol fog-application equipment.

As new technicians, we were trained to conduct cockroach cleanouts by an experienced technician in an on-the-job-type training fashion. As such, the methodologies utilized were subject to the individual who led the field training and varied from what we may have learned in school for a variety of reasons.

At that time, the methodology included using a compressed air sprayer to apply residual insecticides, followed by use of aerosols and ULV applications to flush and kill cockroaches. The liquid residual applications were intended to provide long-term residual control, as well as to assure that cockroaches running from the directed aerosol applications would contact those treated areas as well, in an effort to prevent escape.

Now, what was clearly underestimated during this job was the sheer number of German cockroaches present within that apartment. Note that the previously mentioned *countless thousands* of cockroaches is a comment made with the full benefit of 20-20 hindsight and many years of experience, both of which would have been good to know at *that* time.

With liquid residual applied, it was time to *lay waste* to the cockroaches within the cabinets using directed aerosol applications. So, armed two-fisted with my belt-pack aerosol application system tools, I descended on these unsuspecting cockroaches harboring within the cabinets to wreak my *unholy vengeance* upon them. Well, that was the plan at that time.

Naïveté can be a significant handicap, and what had been classroom-taught can be a somewhat different curriculum than that offered by the school of hard knocks, as it were. Taking careful aim, the intent was to immediately destroy these many cockroaches under a withering field of insecticide aerosol fire. And, armed with baygon- and dursban-based products, I had the good stuff too.

PHOTO 6.4: **The evidence in this kitchen sink flip drawer indicates the level of German cockroach infestation at this apartment. Note the many egg cases present.**

However, the results were slightly different than expected. The 3-D cockroaches were more than anticipated, and the aerosol barrage failed to drop them where they stood, which was readily apparent when cockroaches ran literally everywhere. The situation deteriorated before my very eyes. The cabinet shelves, countertop, floor, ceiling, and adjoining room were soon covered with cockroaches as they ran. Many eventually turned belly up while others simply stopped running. Roaches were climbing up my pant legs, falling off the ceiling on my head and under my collar down my neck beneath my shirt—ah, the good old days. (Of course nowadays we would have simply used a suitable vacuum and immediately removed these cockroaches without making such a mess.)

The din of battle cleared, and eventually there was not a living cockroach to be found, but in seeing the condition of this apartment I simply could not have left this account with so many cockroaches to clean up. Maybe it was my mom's influence or maybe it was just the right thing to do. In any case, the cockroaches needed to be cleaned up, and I decided to do the cleaning myself. However, I had not been properly equipped to do such cleaning and utilized what was available at the account at that time. The supplies available were limited to paper bags, a broom, a dust pan, and a vacuum.

After totally clogging the vacuum full of German cockroaches, the broom and dust pan were next in line. Dead cockroaches were swept into piles and scooped up with the dust

CHAPTER 6: COCKROACH TRIVIA AND RECORDS, UNUSUAL CIRCUMSTANCES, AND WORST-CASE SCENARIOS

pan into a mop bucket. While unsure of the total number of cockroaches, my observation was about three gallons, a large spaghetti pot full of cockroaches, plus whatever was stuffed into the vacuum. Certainly this was a visual image and smell that I have never forgotten after all these years.

PHOTO 6.5: **With experience comes knowledge and wisdom. While vacuuming roaches, nowadays we use professional vacuums such as those available from Atrix Green Supreme and Sierra/Super Coach Pro to immediately remove large quantities of cockroaches from an infested account. Note the white range hood discolored by numerous fecal deposits.**

German Cockroaches

Austin M. Frishman, PhD

When Combat Cockroach Bait was first launched, a national campaign was initiated to seek out the worst cockroach jobs in different parts of the country. People wrote in and explained why they needed help. Once selected, the winners received me for one day along with a local pest-management professional who would follow up the next several months. This was repeated once a year for a few years. Here is one example to give you an idea of how severe the situations were that we encountered.

In a private home in a suburb of Atlanta, the young boy's room had an Atlanta Braves baseball cap sitting on his shelf. As I turned it over, hundreds of cockroaches ran in all directions. His toy Hess trucks had each wheel covered with cockroaches. Every tape deck had a few live cockroaches inside. They had a hamster on a table with a pole touching the ceiling. At night they had a one-way highway of German cockroaches that came out of the attic and devoured the hamster's food.

The owner of the home told me when she fed the dog she stood with a broom to keep the cockroaches away so the dog could eat. You would never know this was the case. The mother worked for the post office and left dressed nicely. On a side note, the technician assigned to help me was a termite technician who thought he wanted to switch into general pest control. It was his first and last job! He switched back to termite work and never tried cockroach management again.

PHOTO 6.6: **Heavily covered monitor traps such as this indicate the level of infestation.**

At a second location the top of a toothbrush was not visible. It was covered with cockroaches—*and this was in the daytime*. When I pulled back the shower curtain, my first impression was that the wall was covered with a dark wallpaper-like surface. As I reached to touch it, it moved. The wall was covered with one massive group of mid-sized to late-instar (nymphal stage) German cockroaches. There were far too many to count. Obviously, one, ten, or twenty tubes of material were not enough to do the job.

American Cockroaches
Paul J. Bello

A hospital had an ongoing American cockroach problem. Of course with MRSA and other such issues, no hospital administrator is going to let a cockroach infestation problem go on for any length of time these days. What was somewhat peculiar was the condition of the newly renovated hospital, the cleanliness of it, and that the presence of cockroaches just didn't seem to fit the physical evidence present during the onsite inspection.

The pest professional had been seemingly doing all the correct things: inspecting, using suitable residual products, sticky traps, and baits, yet the roaches persisted. In a meeting attended by the hospital staff and the pest professional, various subjects were discussed and information was learned about the facility. Of particular interest was the timing of the cockroach sightings, the historical account history data, and the timing of a recent renovation project.

Review and discussion of the pest sighting log revealed the various locations where American cockroaches had been seen. With American roaches we need to consider that they are capable of traveling significant distances from their harborage locations. However, except for a few, the sighting locations seemed to surround the renovated sections of the hospital. One location sightings occurred most often was the dishwashing area within the cafeteria.

When inspecting this area, there was something that seemed weird about it. Brief use of a tape measure indicated that during the renovation work, the contractor had either moved a wall or completely enclosed an area, resulting in a significantly sized hidden void. Note that at times it is easier and less costly to build a wall over or around an existing wall than to remove and rebuild one. As it turned out, this was what had happened here, and the presence of the hidden and inaccessible void area was invisible to those who may not have been familiar with construction.

An inspection through a small access panel revealed a concrete block wall covered with American cockroaches. Once this was determined, it was a rather short time before a suitably sized access panel would be installed and the roach problem was eliminated.

Cockroach Management Work is Important Work:

Certainly our work in eliminating cockroaches from commercial accounts and people's homes is important. Cockroach infestations can build to massive quantities in a short period of time without suitable control efforts being utilized. We believe the stories related here underscore the importance of our industry's work and hope it inspires you to always do your best.

Chapter 7

Non-Chemical Cockroach Control Methodologies and IPM

Perhaps it's fair to say that when bugs unexpectedly appear, most folks reach for the spray can, and the foremost control methodology on people's minds is chemical- or pesticide-based. While this may be so for the general public, with the advent of Integrated Pest Management concepts, techniques, and methodologies, the professional pest management industry has come a long way. In fact, there are many methodologies currently used by the pros that are chemical independent. The professional pest-management industry has seemingly wrapped its collective arms around IPM and non-chemical control methodologies, which this chapter will present.

Vacuums

The use of vacuums to remove cockroaches from an account is a control methodology widely used by pest professionals. Certainly every cockroach immediately removed via vacuum has been removed on a permanent basis from the infested account. When gravid (pregnant) female German cockroaches are removed via vacuuming, the potential population growth may be slowed significantly.

PHOTO 7.1: **Professional vacuums are useful for immediate removal of cockroaches from infested accounts.**

Despite the efficacy of vacuuming, there are some concerns when vacuuming cockroaches. German cockroach infestations have long been known to be associated with allergens that may be problematic for asthma and other pulmonary conditions. These allergens may become airborne and subsequently inhaled by those exposed. As such, care must be taken when using a vacuum to remove cockroaches such that the risk of airborne allergens may be mitigated.

Vacuums used for cockroach control should be either complete HEPA system vacuums or at least be fitted with a HEPA filter. While we may be able to do a sufficient job using a retail shop-type vacuum unit, professional models offer many advantages over their retail counterparts. State-of-the-art HEPA vacuums, such as the professional Atrix Green Supreme or the Sierra/Super Coach Pro models are superior to retail units. These vacuums are complete self-contained HEPA system vacuums used by professionals. Additionally, some of these units are equipped with a canister-type filter located before the motor. When the canister is full, it may be easily removed and replaced as needed.

PHOTO 7.2: **Hand tools are necessary to remove kick plates and access panels for inspection and treatment work. Here, a screw and socket driver kit were used to provide access to the refrigerator motor area.**

Numerous German cockroaches may be removed from infested accounts via vacuuming. These cockroaches tend to aggregate together in certain areas. Knowing where to look, and having a decent LED-type flashlight and a steady hand will go a long way toward successful German cockroach removal. At a typical infested residential account we'd expect to find German cockroaches harboring within kitchen base cabinets, wall cabinets, and pantries. At long-term established infestations there may be hundreds to thousands of German cockroaches present in close proximity to each other, making vacuuming that much more effective.

THE COCKROACH COMBAT MANUAL II

PHOTO 7.3: **A powerful commercial vacuum and LED flashlight are a good combination for cockroach elimination work. Here the vacuum has been fitted with a thin extension tip to allow access to roaches in tight areas.**

Prior to opening your vacuum to empty the cartridge, it is wise to place about one teaspoon of cornstarch on a surface and then sucking it up with the vacuum. Doing so will assure that any possibly live cockroaches within the vacuum will be killed. The cornstarch will clog the spiracles of the cockroaches in the vacuum.

"The thrill of the kill has been replaced by the rapture of the capture," said Dr. Al Green, Government Services Administration. Unfortunately it's not likely that vacuuming alone will eliminate the entire German cockroach population. Additional methods must be used to completely resolve a German cockroach infestation. This is so because they reproduce so quickly and are able to hide in otherwise inaccessible areas.

Steam

With the introduction of professional steam units used for bed bug control by pest professionals, some have adopted their use for cockroach control. However, the efficacy of steamers in cockroach control may be better suited for cleaning surfaces rather than actually destroying the actual cockroaches. Having used steamers to successfully control bed bugs on numerous occasions, we have also worked with steamers in an effort to kill cockroaches.

In working under field locations when steam treating for bed bugs in an infested couch, our observation is that adult German cockroaches are a formidable pest and are difficult at best to kill directly using steam application alone. Note that the younger an immature German cockroach is, the easier it seems to be to kill using direct steam application. However, adult German cockroaches seem to be able to survive the treatment exposure that would kill an immature one.

CHAPTER 7: NON-CHEMICAL COCKROACH CONTROL METHODOLOGIES AND IPM

Steam may be used to flush American cockroaches from floor drains and waste waterlines in commercial accounts. Hundreds of American cockroaches may be flushed from such areas using commercial duty steamers.

One viable use for commercial duty steamers regarding cockroach control may be their use in cleaning and sanitation efforts. These steam machine units are well-suited for cleaning and degreasing soiled surfaces and may be used to clean and remove cockroach feces at certain account locations.

Heat

Pest professionals have been using heat to eliminate bed bugs with great success; however, German cockroaches are more robust and require higher temperatures. While bed bugs may be killed in about one-minute exposure at 122 degrees F, German cockroaches require about seven minutes' exposure at about 130 degrees F. The historical record indicates that the US Army and others have utilized heat to conduct cockroach remediation efforts. At the time of this writing, there are few pest professionals who utilize heat as a practical cockroach elimination tool.

Sticky Traps

While we might argue that cockroaches stuck on sticky traps are in fact eliminated, in a manner of speaking, using sticky traps as a control methodology is likely better suited for investigative and monitoring purposes than for control purposes. However, sticky traps can and do play an important role in cockroach management, as their effective use can help determine the location of hidden harborage areas as well as provide early detection of the presence of cockroaches prior to the occurrence of a significant infestation population. When placed in highly probable locations, sticky traps are extremely efficient as an early warning detection device.

PHOTO 7.4: **It is useful to write the date, number, and location of cockroach sticky trap placements. This information will be useful when following up at an infested account.**

THE COCKROACH COMBAT MANUAL II

PHOTO 7.5: **There are a number of sticky traps commercially available. These traps are cost-effective and help identify cockroach harborage areas.**

Habitat Reduction, Alteration, and Pest Proofing

PHOTO 7.6: **Pest-proofing materials may be used to prevent cockroaches from entering a structure from the exterior or hidden wall voids.**

Like other animals, cockroaches require food, water, and shelter. Limiting or adversely affecting any portion of this survival triangle can have a dramatic effect on the cockroach population at infested account locations. Habitat reduction efforts are geared toward reducing the potential harborage sites available to cockroaches at an account. Doing so places additional stress on the pest population and literally takes away their prime harborage and breeding locations.

There are various means and methodologies with which pest professionals may alter or eliminate the potential harborage locations. As we know, cockroaches prefer cracks and crevices. Such areas may be sealed via the application of suitable caulk and other building materials. Cockroach proofing using caulk and other suitable materials takes away access to hidden areas where cockroaches may breed and build large populations. Areas and items that may be sealed include utility penetrations, light fixtures, countertops, backsplashes, cabinets, sinks, bulletin boards, moldings, and other such areas.

At commercial accounts, the use of cardboard boxes and wood-frame shelves in storage areas has been a long-time hindrance to the cockroach-control efforts of pest professionals. Habitat reduction and alteration efforts call for the discontinued use and avoidance of these cockroach-friendly materials. The use of plastic bags and cockroach-proof storage bins prevents and eliminates harborage areas associated with paper, cardboard, and wooden storage materials.

Over the years we have learned that it's nearly impossible to completely pest proof certain items, such as electronics, commercial motors, etc., despite our best efforts.

Extreme Cold

At a hospital where roaches were a problem, German cockroaches were found harboring in wheelchairs and other items. To eliminate cockroaches, wheelchairs were placed outdoors overnight when the temperature was below ten degrees F, resulting in destruction of the roaches without having to apply pesticides to these sensitive items.

Infested storage containers with contents that could withstand the extreme cold were also placed outdoors overnight to control the cockroaches harboring with them as well. One of the reasons we generally see fewer cockroaches in the winter months is due to the cold temperatures.

However, when servicing infested restaurants in the northeast during winter months, both authors have observed cockroaches exit commercial kitchens to evade the pesticide applications. These roaches would cling to the exterior walls during ULV-type treatments, only to reenter the building at some point after the application work was done.

Sanitation

Cockroaches can survive on very small amounts of food and water. So why is proper sanitation important? It minimizes the total number of cockroaches that can survive in a given area. Food resources limited by sanitation efforts can cause cockroaches to cannibalize their young. Simply stated, proper sanitation reduces the carrying capacity of the area.

Examples of suitable sanitation efforts include but are not limited to

- Removal of excess pet or animal food
- Keeping a tight lid on a trash can
- Use of plastic trashcan liners to avoid spilled food residues
- Not leaving any dirty dishes in the sink at night
- Repair of leaking pipes to prevent water and moisture sources
- Assuring proper seal of refrigerator door seals
- Removal of spilled food debris

- Keeping food containers well sealed
- Avoiding clutter and debris where roaches may harbor
- Avoiding the use of paper bags and cardboard boxes
- Use of regularly scheduled cleaning

Integrated Pest Management or IPM

Nearly every modern-day pest management reference seems to include a discussion of integrated pest-management concepts, or IPM. While some may mistakenly view IPM to mean pest management through the use of no pesticides, IPM actually means the integration of various methodologies in an effort to control, manage, or eliminate a pest, including the use of pesticides. In this chapter we present various non-chemical methodologies that may be implemented to enhance the results of a cockroach management program.

Experienced pest professionals understand that it is unrealistic to assume that successful cockroach control or elimination can be achieved under certain circumstances without the use of efficacious insecticide products. For example, it is unlikely that we would be able to successfully eliminate and manage a significant German cockroach infestation on a long-term basis without the use of residual insecticides and bait products at a reasonable cost.

There is no question that non-chemical control methodologies enhance the overall results of our cockroach management program. Sanitation, proofing work (such as sealing cracks and crevices), vacuuming, and other non-chemical means are useful methodologies. However, these methodologies do not provide long-term or residual protection against subsequent infestation.

Economic Action Threshold Levels

Economic action threshold level is a concept included within IPM. When pest population levels reach a certain level, pest management efforts are implemented to reduce or eliminate the pest in question. These action thresholds make sense when considering crop damage loss versus the cost of pesticide application over many crop acres. There are some who attempt to apply these threshold levels in urban pest management situations. However, these thresholds are better suited to agricultural situations than urban pest situations, which occur in the residential, food production, food service, or other commercial account settings.

Economic pest management action thresholds clearly make sense in the agricultural environment where monitoring pest populations across thousands of crop acres is conducted to trigger pesticide applications in a cost-effective fashion. However, the urban pest professional does not have this option when the threshold level of pests such as German or American cockroaches is essentially constant for every customer at just one individual cockroach. Think of it this way: *How many cockroach sightings would your customers tolerate at their homes or restaurants before they'd call for pest management service?*

PHOTO 7.7: **Due to their great potential breeding ability, the authors agree that even one cockroach in an account is too many.**

Is IPM Well Suited for Cockroach Control?

Certainly IPM has been adopted by many of today's pest professional. Modern pest professionals may be utilizing IPM concepts in their day-to-day operations without realizing it. The use of sanitation, proofing, pest monitors, and regular inspections are all IPM fundamentals. Providing inspection reports that list conditions conducive and corrective recommendations are also fundamental IPM methodologies.

Chapter 8

Insecticides, Resistance, and Cockroach Baits

As pest control technology program students, we learned a lot from Dr. Frishman. What was somewhat amazing were those certain pest control *factoids* that we learned during class, even those that were hard to believe. One such factoid was that if we do monthly service for cockroaches and we kill fewer than 95 percent of the roaches present, when we returned the next month there'd be just as many, if not more, than the previous service visit. Seemed difficult to believe at the time; however, after servicing roach-infested commercial accounts during class field trips, we soon learned it was possible.

As technicians servicing German cockroach-,infested locations we learned the *thrill of the kill* in many ways. Laying waste to thousands of roaches using various chemical tools provided some sort of instant gratification. However, since those days the industry has seen many changes in our modern-day toolbox, techniques, and methodologies. Gone are former industry staple active ingredients such as chlordane, chloropyrifos, baygon, bendiocarb, and diazinon-based products, which have long since been replaced by synthetic pyrethroids, neonicotinoids, and other active ingredient classes of chemistry.

Lack of availability of certain active ingredients of the past has been overcome by improved formulations, equipment, and discovery of new classes of chemistry. Considering the cockroach's ability to develop resistance, such developments are a good and much-needed thing.

Insecticides, Active Ingredients, and Formulations

Pesticides are usually chemical products used to control or eliminate pests. While all insecticides are pesticides, not all pesticides are insecticides. For example, herbicides are pesticides that are used to control or kill weeds, and rodenticides are pesticides used to control or kill rodents. There are also fungicides, avacides, molluscacides, and other pesticides.

Insecticides are pesticide products used to control, manage, or kill insects. Insecticides may be available in various forms or formulation. These products work due to the active ingredient present within the formulation, and the formulation type may vary from

CHAPTER 8: INSECTICIDES, RESISTANCE, AND COCKROACH BAITS

product to product. The type or formulation, class of chemistry of the active ingredient, and the product label language may be key factors in the professional's product selection process.

Pesticide manufacturers screen thousands of chemical compounds each year prior to discovering a compound that will become a development candidate. Few such development candidates progress through the testing process to eventually become a commercially viable product. The cost to bring such a product to market can be a staggering amount, such that the patent period, where the product's manufacturer is protected from copiers, may not seem at all fair to some. Nevertheless, teams of scientists at various manufacturers toil to bring us the latest and greatest insecticide products.

A single active ingredient may exhibit activity against a wide variety of pests. Such broad-spectrum insecticides may be formulated and presented to the market in many products, including dilutable concentrates, directed-spray aerosols, total-release aerosols, ultra-low-volume application insecticides, ready-to-use products, granular insecticides, agricultural insecticide products, turf and ornamental insecticide products, and insect baits. The number of the various insecticide products that share the same active ingredient on a worldwide basis can be surprising. However, for purposes of this book we are only concerned with those insecticide products used for cockroach control.

Dilutable Insecticides

Traditionally, the most competitive and crowded sector of the professional pesticide industry market has been the general-use products. There has always been a copious amount of products available in these type of formulations. Dilutable insecticides are those products that are sold in concentrated form to be mixed with water for subsequent application. There are a number of formulation types that are sold as concentrates, and the various types available warrants discussion.

PHOTO 8.1: **There is a variety of effective concentrate insecticides available for cost-effective cockroach management work.**

Emulsifiable Concentrates

Emulsifiable concentrates, or ECs, are liquid insecticide products that are mixed with water to form a solution. These formulations include emulsifying agents that allow the active ingredient to be mixed with water into a solution that may then be applied using a suitable application device. When mixed, the aqueous solution usually turns white and the solution flows in a similar fashion as would water.

While each formulation may have its own advantages and disadvantages (refer to chart below), ECs are usually relatively inexpensive, and there are many competing products of this type available. An example of an emulsifiable concentrate would be Demon EC and Prelude.

Major Formulation Type (a)	Advantages	Disadvantages
Emuslifiable Concentrates (EC)	Variety of active ingredients. Easy to mix.	May be absorbed by porous surfaces. May stain surfaces. Solvent odors.
Wettable Powders (WP)	Good choice for porous surfaces. Variety of active ingredients.	May wear application equipment. May cause visible residue.
Dusts (D)	Good choice for hidden void treatment. Inexpensive.	Often over applied. Visible residues. Difficult to control drift.
Granular (G)	Easy to apply.	Heavy to handle and store.
Suspension Concentrates (SC)	Effective on most surfaces. Variety of active ingredients. Small particles easily picked up by insects.	May be costly.
Capsulated Suspensions (CS)	Effective on most surfaces. Extended residual.	May be costly.
Baits (B)	Pest specific. Reduced hazard.	Palatable to non-targets. Post application palatability.

(a) This chart does not include all formulation types and the comments are of a general nature. There is no one best formulation for all circumstances.

CHAPTER 8: INSECTICIDES, RESISTANCE, AND COCKROACH BAITS

Wettable Powders

Wettable powders, or WPs, are insecticide products that are formulated as a concentrate powder, as the name implies. A measured amount of the concentrate powder is mixed with water to form a suspension where the powder floats or is suspended within the water. WPs require agitation to assure the proper suspension is maintained and are a good choice when the target area for application is a porous surface. An example of a wettable powder is Tempo WP.

Suspension Concentrates

Suspension concentrates, or SCs, are those insecticide products that, when mixed with water, form a suspension. The suspension is similar to a WP suspension, but the SC may include unique particles such as crystals, which are suspended within the solution rather than a powder. An example of a suspension concentrate would be Temprid SC.

Capsulated Suspensions

Capsulated suspensions are insecticide formulation products that contain micro-capsules that encapsulate the insecticide within the formulation. Capsulated suspensions may also be called micro-encapsulations or MEs. Examples of a capsulated insecticide product are Optem or Demand CS.

Insecticide Dusts

Insecticide dusts are insecticide active ingredients, which are formulated as dry powders or dusts. These dusts are applied using dust application devices or dusters. Dusts are viable cockroach-control products, which are ideally suited for application to hollow voids. Insecticide dusts may contain active ingredients that are traditional insecticide chemicals or natural active ingredients such as

PHOTO 8.2: **A variety of dust insecticides are available to pest professionals for cockroach control.**

boric acid, silica, and other such materials. Examples of a traditional insecticide dust would include Tempo Dust and Alpine Dust. Examples of a natural type dust would include BorActin Dust.

Cockroach Baits

Cockroach insecticide baits have been used for many years. Some of the early bait products were based on active ingredients that are no longer in use. However, some of the earliest successful cockroach bait products were based on boric acid. These boric acid baits were formulated as pastes and tablets, with the pastes being the superior product. Boric acid cockroach baits are still popular and used today.

The next generation of commercial cockroach bait products was Max Force (Combat), which was hydramethylnon. Dr. Frishman played a significant role in the development of Max Force and Combat cockroach products. These baits were primarily used for German cockroaches. Kepone (chlordecone) was an effective American cockroach bait but was removed from the market for environmental concerns.

Modern bait products are effective and based on various active ingredients affording today's cockroach professional a number of options. Today's bait products are formulated as granular baits, gels, and pastes.

PHOTO 8.3: **Dr. Frishman was the primary field researcher in the development project that resulted in the commercialization of Combat cockroach bait.**

PHOTO 8.4: **When first introduced to the professional market, cockroaches quickly came to feed on baits, and some technicians found that roaches could be drawn from their harborages by these baits.**

Granular Insecticides

Granular insecticides are made of particles of certain materials such as corncob, clay, or other material to which insecticides are applied during the manufacturing process. Granular insecticides are mostly formulated for exterior applications but may also be formulated as granular baits. Some granular insecticides may need to be applied prior to rainfall, irrigated, or watered to be an effective application. An example of a granular insecticide is Wisdom Lawn Granular. Examples of granular baits are MaxForce Granular Insect Bait and InVict Xpress granular bait.

Insect Growth Regulators

Insect growth regulators are insecticides by definition but are effective by interrupting the development of the insect. Application of IGRs does not directly result in mortality in the short term but may adversely affect the development, molting, or reproductive process of the insect. Exposure to some IGR products may cause visible malformations, such as twisted wings of cockroaches. Another affect is that some cockroaches are less averse to light after exposure to an insect growth regulator. IGRs can be volatile and may be applied to treat hidden voids as well.

Cockroach Chemical Control Equipment

Generally speaking, cockroach chemical control methodologies include the application of efficacious insecticide products resulting in the demise of cockroach populations. Insecticides of various formulation types may be applied for such purposes using a variety of application equipment designed for this purpose.

A one-gallon, stainless steel, compressed-air sprayer has been a dependable and versatile application device for the pest-management professional. Fitted with specialized tips, the compressed-air sprayer may be used to apply pin-stream, fan-spray, and crack-and-crevice-injection applications, allowing a technician to conduct the lion's share of needed application work at a cockroach-infested account. However, other application equipment devices are also included in the well-equipped professional's toolbox.

Dusts are an important tool in cockroach control and are applied with both hand and power dusters. Ultra low-volume and aerosol fog-generating devices may be used to inject insecticide aerosols into voids as well as conduct a volumetric treatment in large areas to eliminate cockroaches. Bait guns have evolved to deliver precise quantities of cockroach bait.

Cockroach Chemical Control Methodologies

When cockroach control is intended, one of the most effective strategies is to apply residual insecticides to harborage areas. Such areas include hollow voids and tiny cracks and crevices where cockroaches harbor. Typically, the preferred harborage areas are in close proximity to food, water, and sources of heat or warmth. The key for a technician's success is to know and recognize these areas when working at an infested account. The contents within this book will give you an excellent start.

Application to primary cockroach harborage areas, placing insecticides in areas where roaches will assuredly encounter a sufficient toxic dose, is a fundamentally sound strategy. However, because cockroaches may harbor in many areas, both accessible and inaccessible, doing so can be difficult to accomplish.

Cockroach Insecticide Resistance

All too often, when a cockroach population is difficult to eradicate, it is easy to blame it on resistance. When control is difficult to achieve, there may be many factors that come into play that are not related to resistance. In many cases, it comes down to applying the wrong product in the wrong location at the wrong time. It may be that the pesticide was mixed improperly, heat or cold minimized its killing ability, or in the case of baits, it was tainted with other odors before or soon after applied. In the case of cockroaches there can be legitimate resistance whereby over time the cockroaches are no longer killed with the material you know once worked.

This section will explain why and how resistance happens plus a brief history of its occurrence, and, more importantly, what you can do to overcome this situation. As we know, German cockroaches multiply rapidly. Their rapid reproduction enhances their ability to become resistant to pesticides.

Resistance

Generally speaking, there are two types of resistance that are well-known. Behavioral resistance is when the cockroaches exhibit an avoidance of the product. This was problematic as recent as just a few years ago when German cockroaches began to avoid bait products that contained certain components within their bait matrix formulation. Chemical resistance may occur and express itself as a single gene change, or multiple genes are involved.

Determining Legitimate Resistance

First, consider what product used to work to kill the entire population but no longer does. The level of resistance can start out slowly, whereby it is not noticed because enough cockroaches are killed such that it appears as if the control effort has been successful. Then the resistance reaches a level whereby enough individuals survive to breed, thus creating the next generation with a higher percentage of individuals that exhibit the resistance trait. The resistance level can then increase with each successive generation of cockroaches over time.

Resistance then occurs when the same product is used treatment after treatment. In restaurants and other commercial accounts, especially where sanitation is poor, the level of resistance can quickly reach a high level *if* new cockroaches are imported into the account that already exhibit resistance. Therefore, the longer the event exists in the field, the greater the chance cockroaches transported from one area to another will be resistant.

Second, live specimens must be collected and sent to a laboratory equipped to analyze and measure resistance. Over the years it is the technician in the field who usually recognizes the problems first. Some of Dr. Frishman's former students have helped alert us to these problems.

Insecticide Tolerance

Tolerance is *not* resistance. Whatever an individual level of resistance the insect is born with, it remains the same. Tolerance, on the other hand, can increase over the life of that insect. For example, an individual cockroach may become tolerant to colder or warmer temperatures.

How the resistance expresses itself can vary from a morphological change that helps (e.g., thickening exoskeleton) to an altered internal molecular pathway change that cannot be detected simply by looking at the insect.

Dr. Michael Scharf, the O. W. Rollins/Orkin Endowed Chair in Urban Entomology and Molecular Physiology at Purdue University successfully sums up this resistance phenomenon as follows: "Insecticide resistance occurs as a result of four different types of mechanisms or their combinations: biochemical (i.e., a change in the enzymes that degrade insecticides); physiological (i.e., a change in the target site of an insecticide); reduced penetration (i.e., a structural change in the insect exoskeleton that prevents an insecticide from entering the insect's body); and behavioral resistance (i.e., the avoidance of insecticide residues or baits)."

The greater the number of offspring that are produced by an individual female, coupled with the shorter life cycle, increases the chance of selecting a resistant insect or group of insects. If there is no benefit to select for this new trait, it is not selected, and this trait might not reappear again for many generations.

Necessity is the mother of invention. Once resistance is recognized, it drives manufacturers of cockroach-control products to seek solutions and viable product alternatives. This primarily means enhancing or changing existing product formulations.

We learned early in the game that switching from one pesticide to another in the same chemical group is a temporary measure. The reason is simple. Each toxicant has a specific mode of action (method of attack) on the target pests. Some are nerve poisons. Chemists begin to explore new candidate molecules with other avenues of attack. If they select a product in the same chemical group, the insects quickly develop resistance to the new product. This is called "cross resistance." The race is always to find newer chemistry before the existing products fail.

Chemists look *into* the cells to create products that can disrupt insects in new ways. Interestingly enough, most of our current pesticides were initially developed by pharmaceutical companies when developing drugs for humans, livestock, and domestic pets. The well-known product called MAXFORCE or Combat was originally looked at as an anti-malarial drug. It did not work out so well for malaria but proved to work wonders against cockroaches. BASF, Bayer, and Syngenta, all giants in the pharmaceutical industry, are credited with developing excellent products for the urban pest management industry and the public.

Sometimes a manufacturer changes a bait product—not because of any resistance problem, but to increase the speed in which it kills. They do this to try to obtain a competitive edge on their rivals.

A Historical Review of German Cockroach Resistance

We have not seen significant resistance develop in peridomestic cockroach species. This may be because these roaches take much longer to develop and produce fewer offspring when compared to the German cockroach. Cockroach feeding aversion is a behavioral issue and not the same as metabolic resistance to an insecticide.

Once synthetic pesticides were developed and used on German cockroaches, starting in the 1940s, a long history of resistance occurred. With each new chemical group or class of chemistry, hope was initially high but lost its luster over the years. Organochlorine, organophosphate, carbamates, and pyrethroid insecticides have all exhibited varying levels of resistance in German cockroaches.

In 1993, Cockroaches showed feeding-behavior resistance to glucose base gel formulation MAXFORCE baits. The baits were switched to fructose base and began working again.

In 1996, Raid MAX Roach Bait exhibited chemical resistance in some strains of German cockroaches.

Fall 1997, Bayer collected twenty-five different field strains of German cockroaches showing bait aversion. Gel bait aversion cockroaches were slightly smaller, ate less, exhibited a slower reproductive rate (except one strain was faster), and genetically passed the trait on to the next generation.

CHAPTER 8: INSECTICIDES, RESISTANCE, AND COCKROACH BAITS

PHOTO 8.5: **Bait aversion and consumption studies were conducted to determine the most attractive baits for German and other cockroach species.**

The different strains also tested positive to bait aversion on Siege and Avert, two other well-known baits. The field cockroaches tested were collected in the New York tri-state area, Dallas, Fort Worth, areas, and Central Florida.

In 1998 MAXFORCE FC (with Fipronil) was launched. Six months later (May 1999) the first complaints were received from the field.

In December 1999 Dr. Coby Schal of the North Carolina State University Department of Entomology reported on German cockrach resistance to fipronil.

From 1999 to 2002, gel-type cockroach baits were used for many years in accounts where resistance occurred. By early 2003 gel-bait aversion was well documented and publicized in pest-management industry publications.

In 2003 MAXFORCE SELECT was working well.

In 2004 all sugar-based cockroach baits containing fructose, maltose, and sucrose were avoided by many German cockroach populations.

In 2007 Bayer launched MAXFORCE FC Magnum. This bait contains fipronil at 0.05 percent. At this rate the product kills cockroaches that either ingest or contact the product.

Cockroach Baits

At the time of this publication, bait manufacturers seem to have the upper hand on the German cockroach. Over time the cockroaches will likely change and challenge the scientists yet again to come up with another approach.

The current commercially available professional cockroach bait products include products manufactured by Bayer, BASF, Syngenta, and Rockwell Labs as listed below:

Bayer Cockroach Bait Products:

Maxforce FC Roach Killer Bait Stations	0.05 percent Fipronil
Maxforce Select Roach Killer Bait Gel	0.01 percent Fipronil
Maxforce Killer Bait Gel	2.15 percent Hydramethylnon
Pre-Empt Cockroach Gel Bait	2.15 percent Imidacloprid
Maxforce Granular Insect Bait	1.00 percent Hydramethylnon

PHOTO 8.6: **Gel baits such as Maxforce** may be applied to out-of-the-way areas within cabinets and other areas where traditional insecticides might not be used.

CHAPTER 8: INSECTICIDES, RESISTANCE, AND COCKROACH BAITS

BASF Cockroach Bait Products:

Advanced Cockroach Gel Bait	0.5 percent Dinotefuran
Prescription Treatment Alpine Cockroach Gel Bait	0.5 percent Dinotefuran
Avert Dry Flowable Cockroach Bait	0.05 percent Abamectin
Avert Cockroach Bait Stations	0.05 percent Abamectin

PHOTO 8.7: **Cockroach baits such as Advance may be applied to discrete and inaccessible areas where roaches will feed on it.**

Syngenta Cockroach Bait Products:

Advion Cockroach Gel Bait	0.6 percent Indoxacarb

PHOTO 8.8: **Gel baits such as Advion may be applied into shelf supports where roaches can enter and feed.**

Rockwell Labs Cockroach Bait Products:

InVict Gold Cockroach Gel	2.15 percent Imidacloprid
InVict Insect Paste	0.05 percent Abamectin
InTice Roach Bait	30 percent Octoborate acid
BorActin Cockroach granular bait	0.5 percent Boric Acid

PHOTO 8.9: **Cockroach baits such as InVict are often applied to voids behind hinges where roaches harbor.**

Sometimes the cockroaches will advance readily to the gel bait, taste it with their maxillary palpi, and almost snap their head back and walk away. Others will come near the bait, stop, and turn away. Both are signs that you may have a bait-aversion issue.

What Should You Do If Resistance Is Suspected?

- Collect cockroaches to send to an appropriate laboratory for testing.
- Switch to a different bait formulation.
- Supplement the control program with dusts, residuals, and crack-and-crevice-pressurized aerosols.
- Implement sanitation and exclusion measures where possible.
- Utilize non-chemical control measures as detailed in other chapters in this book.
- Monitor with sticky traps and aggressively go after initially low populations that might appear.

The use of cockroach baits has been a long-adopted and successful control strategy for the professional pest-management industry. Since the introduction of Combat, cockroach baits have been successful on the retail market as well. Today's pest professional enjoys a wide variety of cockroach bait products from which to choose. These bait products are available as gels, pastes, and granular formulations, which contain a variety of active ingredients.

Cockroach baits work well for a variety of reasons. It is impossible to find and reach all the hidden harborages in an account, especially if there is clutter. Some of the cockroach baits available today kill slowly. This allows some of the toxicant to pass through the roach's gut and be excreted in their fecal matter. This serves as an additional *bait placement* to harborage areas that have been applied by the roach to these hidden areas. As the young first instar cockroaches feed on these fecal droppings, these roaches will die. The older cockroaches help us by depositing their toxicant-laced fecal matter in the harborage areas. This process is an advantage that baits offer over liquid insecticide applications.

Cockroach Baiting Practical Tips

Practical cockroach baiting tips are presented here for your review and consideration.

- Based upon your inspection and the infestation level observed, determine if using cockroach baits is a viable strategy for the account.
- Use a sufficient amount of bait to adequately address the cockroach population present.
- Consider the service frequency and scheduled follow-up when conducting bait applications.
- Be selective where baits are placed. Avoid simply caulking the entire cabinet with your bait application.

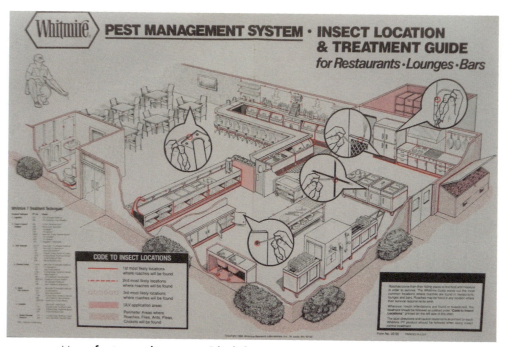

PHOTO 8.10: **Manufacturers have provided the pest management industry with useful training aids such as this restaurant inspection and application guide produced by Whitmire in 1984 and presented here thanks to BASF.**

THE COCKROACH COMBAT MANUAL II

- Place cockroach baits in out-of-the-way, difficult-to-see, and difficult-to-access locations.
- Consider the use of cardboard hollows and other such materials or objects for cockroach bait placements rather than simply direct application to cabinet interiors.
- For baits to be consumed by cockroaches, the bait must get past the cockroach's taste receptors located in two sets of palpi and within its oral cavity.
- Store your baits in sealed containers away from other pesticide products to avoid possible tainting.
- Do not smoke when handling or applying cockroach baits.
- Do not mix other pesticides near or when handling cockroach baits.
- Avoid storing baits in areas of extreme temperatures.
- Always use fresh baits. Using old baits may save you money in the short run but waste your labor time in the long run if not palatable to the roaches.
- Only use those cockroach bait tubes that are compatible with your applicator gun and vice versa.
- In warm climates and on hot days, avoid storing your baits in a hot vehicle. Excessive heat may cause your baits to run when applied. It may be wise to use a small insulated cooler to store your baits when on the road.
- Learn how to use your bait applicator gun correctly.
- Do not force your bait applicator gun, as this may damage parts.
- Do not apply where children and pets may access the bait.
- Do not apply insecticides in areas near bait placements.
- When application of residual insecticides may be done in combination with cockroach bait applications, avoid application of insecticides in close proximity to areas to be baited, and wait until insecticide applications have dried prior to bait application.

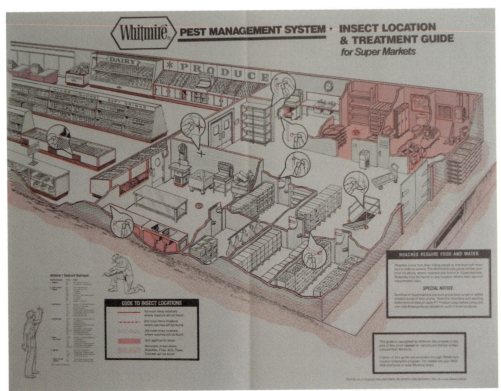

PHOTO 8.11: **The above Super Market service guide was created by Whitmire in 1984 and presented here courtesy of BASF.**

CHAPTER 8: INSECTICIDES, RESISTANCE, AND COCKROACH BAITS

- If you open a kitchen cabinet and find numerous cockroaches present, it may be better to use a vacuum to immediately remove many of the insects rather than to simply apply bait and wait for them to feed on your applications. Doing so will deliver some immediate relief to the customer while reducing the number of roaches, which need to feed on your bait placements to attain full control.
- Use paper peel-and-stick dots or labels to indicate where bait tray placements are located. This is especially useful when baits are placed in drop ceilings.
- Place bait trays in corners such that wall surfaces will funnel roaches toward your bait placements.
- Initially vacuum high numbers of cockroaches prior to installing bait trays and placements. If not, the roaches may use your stations as harborages rather than feeding and defecate on your baits, rendering them ineffective.
- Be sure the back of bait trays is placed against the wall surface or flush with the surface it is resting upon.
- Place baits on horizontal and vertical surfaces.
- Place baits in the isolated zones present at the account. For example, each cabinet may be an isolated zone that is inaccessible from the neighboring cabinet. If this is the case, each separate cabinet or zone must be baited.
- Store baits in sealed Ziploc bags to avoid contamination and odors from other pesticide products.
- Keep baits out of reach of children, mentally challenged individuals, and pets.

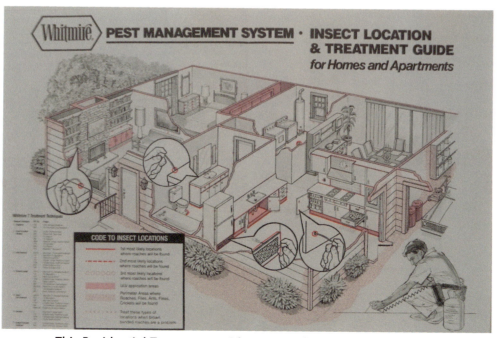

PHOTO 8.12: **This Residential Treatment guide was produced by Whitmire in 1984 and presented here courtesy of BASF.**

- Avoid bait placements in areas containing excessive temperatures such as steam pipes, areas of high humidity, and other heat sources as baits may grow mold and become unpalatable.

- Wrap bait containers prior to disposing and dispose of per label instructions.
- Place a thin layer of petroleum jelly atop bait trays and stations to prevent people from stealing your bait placements. This is pertinent in some commercial account locations.
- Use sticky traps to help you determine the best locations for bait placements.
- In dusty environments, place baits within paper, folded within cardboard, or within cardboard tubes to protect the bait from becoming overly soiled. Use a rubber band to secure the bait.
- To be optimally effective, the bait must be located between the cockroach harborage and their feeding areas.
- Sanitation—the removal of food debris—enhances the acceptance and feeding of bait placements.
- When applying gel bait to cracks and crevices, do not fill the area. Leave room for the roach to get in and feast on your bait.
- Avoid areas where the temperature will exceed one hundred degrees F, as baits will run.
- Use many small placements for German cockroaches.
- Use larger placements for American cockroaches.
- Remove old, dried baits when possible.
- Do not fill cockroach bait stations with gel baits. Think of these stations as *tanks*, and the gel placements as infantry scattered around the protective area.
- Do not apply liquid or aerosol insecticides atop bait placements.
- Use bait applicator extension tubes to apply baits in hard to reach areas.
- Watch for a few seconds to see if cockroaches respond to your bait placements. If not, you may be applying in the wrong area, using the wrong bait, or there may be behavioral resistance to this type of bait.

Chapter 9

Killing Cockroaches with Insecticides

As professionals, our goal is to eliminate cockroaches for our customers. The use of pesticides plays an important role in attaining this goal. For the most part, the professional pest control market has a wide variety of insecticide product options available with which to kill cockroaches. Manufacturers of such products may refer to this market segment as the *general-use insecticide* product market. The commercially available products in this segment include aerosols, dilutable concentrates, and dusts. It is a somewhat crowded market, with many active ingredients, formulations, and products available.

A number of highly effective insecticide products are commercially available.

Back in the sixties and seventies, the professional market was dominated by the older chemistries: chlorinated hydrocarbon, such as chlordane, organophosphate, and carbamate insecticides. By the late seventies and into the eighties, cockroaches became more difficult to control with these insecticides, and resistance was a concern. Concerns regarding organophosphate pesticides set the clock ticking on this class of chemistry. Yet all the while, cockroaches endured and issues with cockroach control increased.

A Game-Changer Arrives

Around 1985, ICI (which became Zeneca and is now Syngenta) developed and launched the product Demon into the professional market. Demon was one of the initial synthetic pyrethroid-based liquid insecticide products launched targeting the professional cockroach market, and it's fair to say it was a game changer. Demon contained the active ingredient cypermethrin. Many a technician dealing with tough cockroach situations during the late eighties and into the early nineties will tell you "he knocked the tar out of roaches" using Demon.

The professional pest market reacted quickly, and soon a number of synthetic pyrethroids joined cypermethrin on the shelves. These pyrethroids included permethrin-, bifenthrin-, and cyfluthrin-based products to which roaches succumbed likely by the billions. However, as time marched on so did the cockroach, and the roaches had ideas of their own. Over time, cockroaches began to develop resistance to the pyrethroid products. Seemingly overnight the industry found that cockroaches became tougher to control.

Cockroach-Control Chemistry

Global basic manufacturers are those companies that discover and develop proprietary compounds formulated into brand name pesticide products. They usually own, manufacture, and are referred to as being *basic* in their active ingredient products. The total number of these companies has diminished over the past twenty years. Current global basic manufacturers include BASF, Bayer, and Syngenta. These companies are also amongst the largest in the world and employ numerous scientists who are constantly working to refine current and develop new efficacious products for control of cockroaches and other target pests. They have to continue these efforts; they don't have a choice. If they rest on their laurels, the cockroaches and their competitors will soon enough pass them buy.

During the heyday of pyrethroid products, the manufacturers worked diligently to create and develop more effective insecticides. New classes of chemistry became available in formulated products to pest-management professionals. Bayer was the first to hit the market with the neonicotinoid imidacloprid. Soon after came a phenylpyrazole, fipronil, which was followed by an oxadiazine introduction. Thanks to the work of chemical engineers, formulation chemists, and entomologists, the pest-management industry has excellent weapons available with which to successfully battle cockroaches.

Today's cockroach service technician has a wide variety of cost-effective aerosols, liquid concentrates, dusts, and granular insecticide products from which to choose. Each of these registered products has been extensively refined and tested prior to becoming available to the professional market. It is important that applicators understand how this product-development work relates practically to their pest-control fieldwork.

Potential pesticide products progress through a complex development process. The manufacturers spend countless hours of research and tens of millions in development dollars to successfully produce an effective pesticide product. Many tests and refinements occur prior to the product's appearance on the distributor's shelves. One of the most important aspects of this extensive product development process are those tests that determine the concentration and application rates for the product. Simply stated, by the time the product becomes commercially available, it has been extensively tested to determine the optimal cost-effective rate of application for the labeled pest.

Experienced applicators know that they should *always read and follow pesticide label directions*. They should also appreciate that the manufacturers of these pesticide products have invested many countless hours and vast resources to determine the optimal application rates and directions that appear on the product label.

Selecting the Proper Pesticide Product

With numerous pesticide products to choose from, selecting the best product for you can be a challenge. There are a number of factors that should be considered prior to making the purchase selection. Such factors include product efficacy, label language, and cost.

While each of these factors may be important considerations, practically speaking, the most important consideration is likely the pesticide label language. Assuming acceptable product efficacy, the individual pesticide product label language is a critical factor for today's discerning pest professional for many reasons. Label use directions and restrictions therein catch the keen eye of the pest professional during the product selection process. Where and how a pesticide product may be applied and for which pests are important considerations. Application frequency and application rate specifications for the target pest are also key considerations. When selecting between two products, the one with the better label language may often be the better choice.

However, comparing products by cost alone is more difficult than it may appear on the surface. The wise pest professional knows to compare competing product costs under like conditions to determine fair, reasonable, and true comparison results. Such comparisons might include application cost for the target pest in question, cost per finished gallon, and application cost per thousand square foot. The labeled rate for the target pest in question must also be suitably considered so an accurate comparison can be made because the competing products may have different application rates that would affect final application cost. When comparing competing products, consider like parameters for the target pest, the label rate, the cost per treated area, application restrictions, application frequency, and other such factors.

Pesticide Applications

The best common-sense rule when properly applying insecticides was imparted to me by a savvy industry veteran many years ago when we were chatting at an industry meeting. He succinctly summed up this concept when he said, "You gotta get the bug juice where the bugs are"—and he was correct. Simply stated, we're not going to successfully control cockroaches in the kitchen by applying the best product available in the bedrooms.

For optimal control, the technician must match application methodologies to the target cockroach species' biology and behavior. It is best to apply insecticide products to harborage areas where roaches tend to spend most of their time, as well as along hidden voids and travel paths so insecticide residues will be encountered by the roach. To attain control, we must place our residual products where the roaches will interact with them.

Dust Applications

The professional pest-management industry has been using dust insecticides for many years. Typically, dusts are desiccants, such as diatomaceous earth or silica gel or toxicant dusts, which contain various active ingredients. Dusts are amongst the least costly insecticide formulation products and offer a cost-effective treatment option because just a small amount of dust seems to go a long way. Insecticide dusts are ideal for treating hidden void areas where cockroaches may harbor and travel. There are some logistical challenges that must be overcome when applying insecticide dusts.

Insecticide dusts are available with a variety of active ingredients, from natural exempt-type products to traditional insecticide active ingredients. The applicator should understand the expected performance of the dust product selected and choose the dust product that best matches the needs of the account where applied.

A little dust goes a long way. Dusts must be carefully applied, and the tendency to over-apply should be avoided. While technicians may intend to apply dust into a crack or crevice, doing so without having excess dust on the surrounding surface is difficult to accomplish. However, applications are better suited to treat hidden voids where the application can provide superior coverage than a liquid application as the dust floats and settles on the surfaces within the void.

There are many voids within a cockroach-infested account where dusts may be successfully applied. Examples include wall voids surrounding utility penetrations, hollows beneath base cabinets, hollows behind cabinet and fixture kick plates, masonry wall voids, voids behind cabinets, and other such areas. Care must be taken to avoid over-application to areas outside the intended treatment location. Excess dust should be removed should this occur. There are also situations where dusts are a poor choice, including flammable areas due to risk of explosion, dirty and dusty areas where the dust may be coated by non-toxic debris, in suspended ceilings where the dust may fall from the application area, and around certain electrical equipment where the motor cooling fan may move or translocate the dust. When applying dust to electrical outlets and other such areas, care should be taken to avoid contact with live electrical wires.

Dusts are the least-costly pesticide formulation type and may be applied with inexpensive application devices as well. Applicators may choose from hand-bellows-type dusters to more costly electronic power dusters. Despite which application device is used, the technician must learn how to use the device to properly apply insecticide dust. An advantage of dust applications is that as the roaches travel through a treated area, the dust clings to their feet, antennae, and other body parts. It is then ingested by the cockroach during the preening or cleaning process.

Aerosol Applications

Perhaps no other form of insecticide formulation offers more convenience than aerosols for cockroach control. This is so because aerosols do not require mixing or additional equipment to apply. They may be applied in various ways to various areas, including cracks, crevices, hollow voids, spots, and surfaces, and the can be discarded when completely used. Aerosols are also available with a variety of active ingredients, providing choices for the professional.

PHOTO 9.2: **Ready-to-use aerosol insecticide products are available with a variety of active ingredients labeled for use against cockroaches.**

While aerosol cans offer unique application options, including space-spray application, surface application, and application injection tip, aerosols may also deliver insecticides as liquid, mist, or foam applications. Injection-tip aerosols and application belt-pack systems are useful when treating cracks and crevices for cockroaches in both residential and commercial accounts.

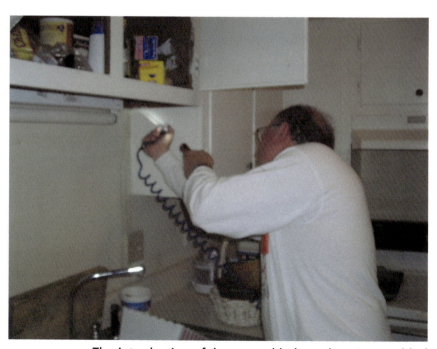

PHOTO 9.3: **The introduction of the aerosol belt-pack systems added convenience to the use of aerosol products.**

Aerosol ready-to-use (RTU) cans are formulated to contain various active ingredients that are effective against cockroaches. Some aerosol cans may contain a combination of active ingredients as well. Many aerosols are labeled for food handling and residential and commercial account use, which affords the pest professional many options.

THE COCKROACH COMBAT MANUAL II

Concentrate Insecticides

Concentrate insecticides are mixed with water and applied using compressed air and other application equipment. They offer great flexibility in active ingredient selection, formulation type, target pests, and application methodology. These products are highly efficacious against cockroaches.

Concentrate insecticides may provide residual and immediate control of cockroaches when applied in accordance with label directions. Care should be taken to read and understand the label mixing and application instructions to ensure the appropriate concentration is mixed and applied.

Concentrate insecticides may be applied using a number of equipment options. The one gallon, stainless steel, compressed-air sprayer has been a professional pest-management industry staple since its introduction in the 1950s. When well cared for and maintained, the compressed-air sprayer will reward its owner with many years of dependable service life. However, dilutable concentrate insecticides may be applied with other types of equipment as well. Trigger pump sprayers, electric sprayers, and ULV-generating units may also be used to apply these products.

PHOTO 9.4: **Liquid concentrate insecticides are applied with compressed air sprayer and are available in a variety of formulation and active ingredients. Note the presence of hand tools, aerosols, duster, and professional vacuum all used during this cockroach work.**

PHOTO 9.5: **Professionals have learned the advantages of using ULV generating devices such as an Actisol to apply water-based dilutable insecticide products.**

As with other cockroach insecticide products, it is important to apply these insecticides to the appropriate locations to deliver an effective cockroach-control application. Practical application tips are provided at the end of this chapter.

Insect Growth Regulators

Insect growth regulators (IGRs) are insecticide products that effect the development of the insect. These IGRs work by disrupting insect molting or other development processes. IGRs are classified as either chitin synthesis inhibitors or juvenoids. They are effective tools when cockroach insecticide resistance is a concern and may be used alone or in combination with residual insecticides. Volatile IGRs may reach roaches harboring in hidden areas. Some IGRs are more effective against insects that develop with complete metamorphosis than those with gradual metamorphosis. Cockroaches develop via gradual metamorphosis, so it is wise to choose an IGR that is better suited for use against cockroaches.

Granular Insecticide Application

Granular insecticide products may be formulated as both baits that the cockroaches ingest or as insecticides that kill when the cockroach comes in contact with the granule or the residual thereof. Insecticide granules are available with a variety of active ingredients that may be used to control cockroaches. Typically granule insecticides are used to control the larger cockroaches, including American, Oriental, Smokey brown, Turkistan, and other such cockroaches. Note that some of these cockroach species are found both inside and outside structures.

It is best to apply granule insecticides using suitable application equipment such as a spreader. Care must be taken to calibrate the spreader for the granular product applied so the proper amount is applied in compliance with the label directions.

Practical Tips For Cockroach Control Insecticide Applications

- Always read, understand, and follow pesticide label directions.
- Mix the amount of pesticide to be applied, and apply what has been mixed.
- Location is of critical importance to your application success. Apply the suitable insecticide to the areas where cockroaches harbor and travel.
- At a residential account, areas where German and other cockroaches normally harbor may include under cabinets; cracks and crevices within and between cabinets; in cabinet door hardware; cabinet drawer hardware; behind moldings and trim; in refrigerator and large appliance motors; along and in refrigerator door weather stripping; within the hollow insulated panels of stoves and ovens; within ranges and cook tops; within pantries; near plumbing; near leaks; near food and water sources; beneath countertops; within clocks and other wall hangings; within utility outlets and table and chair framework; along door and window molding; within small and large appliances; around and under sinks; pantry shelves; dishwashers; trash cans; recycle cans; pet food storage containers; door hinges; televisions;

television cabinets; bulletin boards; plants; shelves; framed art and decorative items; window shades and blinds; toasters; coffee makers; night stands; dressers; wardrobes; drawers; can openers; knife storage racks; cardboard and paper; wall voids; curtains; medicine cabinets; toilets; and many other places.

- Apply dusts to areas including utility penetrations, hollow wall voids, masonry wall voids, and other such areas where roaches may harbor and travel.
- Apply residual insecticides to cracks and crevices, under countertops, and within cabinets where cockroaches may harbor.
- Do not apply residual insecticides near or over cockroach bait applications.
- IGRs may be tank mixed with residual insecticides.
- Ensure that the insecticide product applied is suitably mixed, agitated, and fresh. Avoid storing pesticide within your sprayer overnight or over the weekend.
- Note that IGRs may alter normal behavior of cockroaches and cause them to be less averse to light. This could cause roaches to become more visible.
- Cockroaches exposed to IGRs often display certain visible malformations such as twisted wings, which is the most common. Some customers may think that this could affect them; however, IGRs only affect insects that molt. Humans do not molt.

PHOTO 9.6: **It is necessary to remove outlet covers to provide access for treatment in hidden wall void areas where cockroaches may harbor.**

Chapter 10

Application Equipment Use and Care

Long-term successful, professional cockroach control cannot be accomplished without the use of suitable professional equipment. The fundamental equipment is common to nearly all pest professionals and includes application, inspection, and accessory-type equipment. In this chapter, practical tips are presented after each category of equipment rather than at the end of the chapter.

Flashlights

The flashlight is a critical tool for any pest professional. There have been great advances in flashlight technology in the recent years due to LED technology. The flashlights available today provide excellent light and long-term battery light at reasonable prices. In fact, the flashlights available today from nontraditional professional brand name manufacturers are serious competitors in the flashlight market.

- LED-type flashlights provide superior light to traditional flashlights.
- LED flashlights are now available at reasonable prices from a variety of sources.
- LED flashlights are available in rechargeable and regular battery-type units.
- LED upgrade bulbs are available at reasonable cost to retrofit your traditional flashlight bulb.
- Always have a backup flashlight on hand when working in the field, just in case.
- Always keep spare batteries on hand when working in the field.
- LED headlights provide good lighting and the advantage of hands-free working ability.

PHOTO 10.1: **The pest-management industry has benefited from the significant advances in flashlight technology. Today's flashlights are brighter and energy efficient, and high-quality flashlights may be purchased at a reasonable cost.**

THE COCKROACH COMBAT MANUAL II

Hand Tools

Today's pest-control professional is called upon by customers to provide professional services in a variety of settings and situations. Of fundamental concern is the required access for inspection and successful pest-elimination services. Oftentimes various hand tools are needed to provide access as well as to conduct minor equipment repairs while in the field. As such, pest professionals are well advised to keep an adequately provisioned toolbox to meet such needs.

- A well provisioned toolbox with quality workmanship is a good investment.
- Assure that your toolbox includes the proper sized and type tools that you need to service your application equipment in the field when necessary.
- Only purchase high-quality tools. The savings experienced buying "cheap tools" may cost you plenty later when they are actually needed on the job.
- Typical tools needed to create access for cockroach treatment service include but may not be limited to screwdrivers, pliers, pry bar, wrenches, drills, drill bits, electric screwdrivers, screwdriver bits, Allen wrenches, and other such tools.
- Keep an inventory of tools within the box and replace tools as needed.
- Include a twenty-five-foot tape measure. Use this to determine the presence of inaccessible, or *blind*, hidden voids within structures where cockroaches may harbor.
- Use a toolbox that may also be used as a stepstool.

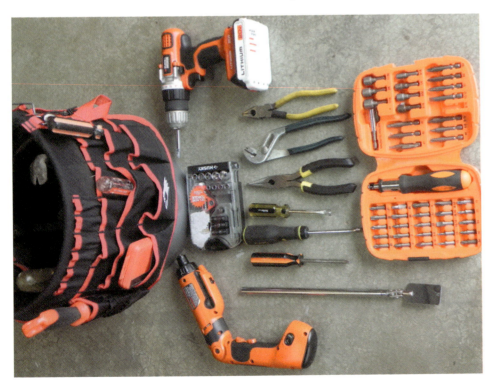

PHOTO 10.2: **A well-prepared technician is equipped with a variety of hand tools needed to create access for cockroach inspection and service work.**

Compressed-Air Sprayer

Assuredly the one gallon, stainless steel, compressed-air sprayer has been the long-term standard of the pest-professional industry. These sprayers are designed in a simple fashion. They work by use of air pressure, which basically pushes the insecticide solution down, up the siphon tube, and out the spray nozzle.

The one gallon compressed-air sprayer offers the pest professional flexibility in application due to the multiple application tips. These tips give the applicator the choice of fine-pin stream, heavy-pin stream, fine flat fan spray, coarse flat fan spray, and crack-and-crevice-injection application. Simply stated, the one gallon sprayer can be used for nearly any cockroach control job and may be responsible for the demise of more cockroaches than any other type of application equipment.

As dependable as the compressed air sprayer may be, it is neither *bulletproof nor idiot proof*. The technician's favorite sidekick requires suitable care and maintenance to remain as dependable as expected. The pest professional should refer to the owner's manual for recommendations on acceptable use patterns and practices. However, even with normal use, certain parts wear out and must be replaced in a timely fashion.

PHOTO 10.3: **A common problem that is easily remedied is a clogged strainer screen in a compressed-air sprayer.**

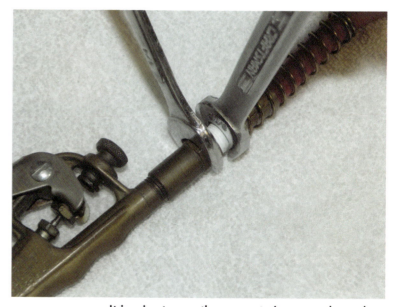

PHOTO 10.4: **It is wise to use the correct-size wrenches when performing maintenance work on your compressed-air sprayer.**

PHOTO 10.5: **A cleaned strainer screen.**

Parts that require regular maintenance and replacement include the packings, gaskets, check valve, plunger cup, strainer screen, shut-off valve seat, hose, and others. Review of the owner's manual troubleshooting guide will enable the technician to understand reasons his sprayer is not functioning properly and offer a suitable remedy. In the event that your sprayer fails to operate properly, refer to your manual.

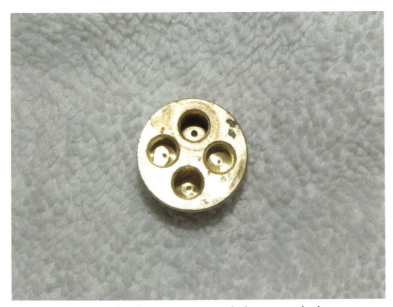

PHOTO 10.6: **Inspect the four-way tip and clean regularly.**

PHOTO 10.7: **Inspect the pump gasket regularly and replace when needed.**

- Keep your compressed-air sprayer clean.
- Avoid storing pesticide solution within your sprayer overnight or over the weekend.
- In northern climates, be sure to completely drain your spray wand to avoid freezing, which would damage it.
- Only use clean, clear water in your sprayer.
- Keep an extra supply of fresh water on hand to refill your sprayer as needed.
- Have proper-sized wrenches on hand with which to service your sprayer. Avoid using pliers to loosen nuts or dismantle a sprayer wand or hose. Doing so may permanently damage the nuts.
- If your sprayer will not spray and appears clogged, relieve the pressure and check the strainer screen. Note that you will need properly sized wrenches to accomplish this.
- Strainer screens may be successfully cleaned if need be. However, keep a spare strainer screen on hand for quick replacement if need be.
- Change sprayer gaskets and compression packings periodically as needed so your sprayer is always ready for work.
- Keep a dated service log for your sprayer so normal wear items are serviced and replaced on your schedule rather than as a result of breakdown or failure in the field.

Dusters

Dust application equipment can be simple and easy to use. The typical bellows-type duster is squeezed so a puff of air is created to carry the dust down the application tube to the target site. Proper application of dust requires just a small amount. Perhaps the most common dust-application error is when the applicator holds or positions the duster so the tube is at the bottom, which over-applies the dust. Remember: *less is more*.

- Battery-powered dusters are used by some professionals and can be useful for large jobs where dust must be applied to many areas.
- Dust applicators may be fitted with extension pipes and hoses that allow application of difficult-to-reach areas. Additionally, it is especially wise to place a plastic-type hose, such as a fish-tank hose, on the tip of the applicator to insulate from potential electrical shock.
- Avoid overfilling your duster.
- Place marbles or ball bearings inside your duster to help keep the dust from clogging and to keep it ready for application.
- Hold your duster right-side up when applying dust insecticides.
- Avoid over-application.
- Do not apply dusts in overly wet or dirty environments.
- Avoid application in areas where people may subsequently encounter the dust.
- Choose the product most suitable for the account situation.
- Have a set of spare batteries on hand for your power duster.

ULV Generating Injection Devices

Ultra-low volume generating injection devices are a useful tool for cockroach control. These units are ideal for injection treating cracks, crevices, and void areas where cockroaches harbor and travel. They offer the applicator the advantage of deep-penetrating application ULV mist that is pushed into target areas where needed by forced air from the treatment nozzle. Additionally, many of the liquid concentrate insecticide products may be applied using these devices, making such applications cost-effective for the applicator. Care should be taken to

PHOTO 10.8: **The Actisol has been a dependable and superior ULV injection application device for many years.**

avoid mixing water-based products with oil-based products due to solution compatibility issues.

- Keep your ULV machine clean and ready to work.
- Avoid leaving insecticide residue inside your ULV machine overnight.
- Completely empty your ULV machine when finished use.
- Use the appropriate-sized extension cord to power your ULV unit.
- Care must be taken when ULV application treatments must be done in areas where there may be open flames such as pilot lights.
- Air currents may cause the ULV mist to be diverted frm the area of intended treatment.
- Elevator shafts may have an updraft or downdraft which needs to be considered prior to treatment. Additionally, some elevators may have dual doors that open to the service as well as non-service areas which may require suitable securing prior to treatment work.
- Use of residual treatment applications in combination with ULV treatment may be needed to adequately address any areas where roaches might otherwise escape ULV type applications. Be sure that such residual treatment is approved for the account prior to such applications.

Chapter 11

Special Situations

Cockroaches are an *equal-opportunity infester*. No structure inhabited by man is immune to a cockroach infestation. The pest-management industry has a long-established, persistent, and wily adversary that seemingly defeats some of our best efforts. While it's fair to say that the cockroach is one of the industry's most significant foes, in many ways roaches represent long-term job security for the pest professional.

This chapter presents discussions and practical tips for certain types of accounts. Each section is followed by practical tips that are useful for that type of account but may be equally useful in other account situations as well.

Hospitals and Health-Care Facilities

Even health-care facilities, where a sterile, clinical environment is expected, can become infested with cockroaches. With the presence of numerous patients and the potential mechanical transmission of pathogens, roaches are an unwelcome guest at any health-care facility. The pest-management professional plays an important role in disease prevention.

Health-care facilities present unique challenges to the pest-management professional. Concerns regarding the necessity of a sterile environment, accessibility, and the careful use of select insecticide products are factors that must be considered. Where there is

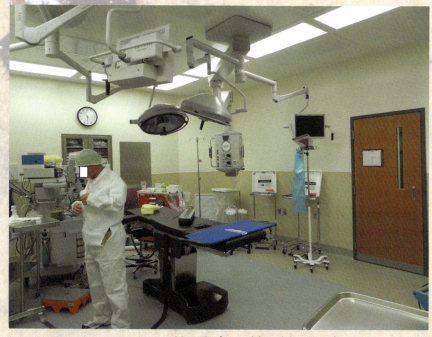

PHOTO 11.1: **Hospitals and health-care facilities present unique challenges to the pest professional.**

restricted accessibility to areas of concern during normal working hours, conduction of normal pest-management work may not be possible in the presence of patients and even vehicle parking. Such logistical factors must be considered by the pest professional.

Depending on the type of health-care facility being serviced, there may be additional factors to consider prior to initiating the work. A large hospital will have diverse environs and types of account locations all present within the same large facility. Such account types present may include patient rooms; surgical suites; administration offices; locker rooms; bathrooms; food service areas; kitchens; storage areas; parking decks; waiting rooms; reception areas; pharmacy; morgue; various clinical areas such as radiology; cardiology; oncology; maternity; pediatrics; orthopedics; and many others. Add a cockroach problem, and it's fair to say that each of these areas presents its own unique challenges.

PHOTO 11.2: **Hospitals require the technician to be prepared to service all areas.**

Following are practical tips relative to cockroach control in health-care facilities.

- No health-care facility is immune to cockroach introduction and infestation. German, American, and Oriental cockroach infestations occur at health-care facilities.
- Large health-care facilities may have a sanitarian, risk management, and/or safety manager who is responsible for pest management. The pest professional must learn who all the key contact personnel are and include them in necessary communications.
- Large facilities may be broken down by area for scheduling of service work.
- Maintain a service and pest sighting logbook on site at a designated location.

- The service log book should include:
  - A description of the service protocol for the account, including a list of pests covered under the normal service agreement.
  - A pest-sighting log
  - Service-request log
  - A service schedule
  - Copies of completed service sheets
  - Key contact information for the account and the pest professional providing service
  - An emergency service telephone number
  - A list of approved products and methodologies
  - Specimen labels and MSDS (OSHA-regulated safety data sheets) for each of the approve product materials
- Carefully select the products and methodologies to be implemented in your cockroach-control program. Discuss and explain these options with the suitable manager of the health-care facility.
- Carefully consider the situation prior to the application of pesticides within a health-care facility. When roaches must be eliminated from sensitive areas such as patient rooms, surgical procedure, and other sterile rooms, consider the use of vacuums and other insecticide-free solutions.
- When servicing large facilities, it is reasonable to request vehicle parking and suitable onsite supply/equipment storage be made available for the pest professional.
- Request a simple map of large facilities that may be used for service scheduling and to identify locations of various control device installations.
- Ensure that service technicians wear a suitable uniform with identification badges.
- Ensure that suitable access is provided to all areas requiring inspection and service.
- Provide the facility with written recommendations to correct conditions conducive to pests noted during the regular service inspections.
- Provide the facility with written recommendations on suitable prevention procedures that the facility staff can implement to enhance the results of the overall pest-management program.
- Provide suitable training sessions for facility staff as part of the annual service contract.
- Obtain a list of key contact personnel for each area being serviced.
- Identify and map areas of concern for cockroach control including floor drains; sewer line locations; utility chase areas; food service and storage areas; trash compactor; laundry; shipping/receiving area; elevator shafts; food vending machines; coffee shop or snack bar area; coffee break areas; and other such areas.
- Place monitor/sticky traps and indicate on map in key locations.
- Assure monitor traps are numbered and dated when placed.
- Record cockroach activity observed in monitor traps.
- Identify any inaccessible areas that require inspection and service. Recommend the installation of access panels where necessary.

Restaurants and Food Handling

Restaurants and food-handling facilities are constantly at risk of cockroach infestation. These accounts typically have numerous delivery arrivals that can introduce roaches on a daily basis. The greater the amount of food prepared and/or served at the account, the greater the risk of a cockroach introduction and resulting infestation. Within such accounts are a number of micro-environs that must be inspected and serviced to prevent and remediate cockroaches. From shipping/receiving areas to the trash compactor area and all points in between, each presents challenges for the pest professional.

PHOTO 11.3: **Food-handling accounts may have drop ceilings requiring inspection and service work. The well-equipped technician has a suitable ladder for such service work.**

The experienced and competent pest professional is attune to the concerns of the restaurant and food-handling account customer. While large food-handling accounts may employ a sanitarian and have a master chef who runs the kitchen operations, at a local family-run restaurant, the chef, owner, and general manager may be the same person. No matter the size or nature of the food-service account, one thing is for certain: cockroaches are a constant threat and an unwelcome visitor. The food-handling industry relies on pest professionals to keep their business locations cockroach free.

PHOTO 11.4: **Retail food service requires service to be conducted in a discrete fashion and often during *off or after hours*.**

Following are practical tips relative to cockroach control in restaurant and food-handling facilities for your review and consideration.

- Scheduling of service should match the needs of the type of account being serviced. While food preparation and manufacturing facilities may be serviced at nearly any time during the day, a restaurant must be serviced when the dining public is

CHAPTER 11: SPECIAL SITUATIONS

not present, and many restaurants may prefer pest management services to be conducted at night.
- Understandably, one of the most significant concerns of a restaurant manager is a guest sighting a live cockroach in the dining room. Restaurants are reliant upon the pest professional to prevent this from happening.
- Avoid the use of flushing insecticides in restaurant locations.
- Cockroach control work conducted in public dining areas must be discrete.
- Food courts in shopping malls may have many individual vendors all located in close proximity. In such circumstances a cockroach infestation may quickly spread from one to another.
- The experienced pest professional knows that food courts, where there are a number of food service vendors present, are ideally serviced by the same pest professional at the same time.
- Use monitor traps to identify problem areas prior to a significant infestation occurring.
- It is critical to find and treat the harborage areas to successfully control the cockroach problem at the account. Even the best products will not eliminate the roach problem if applied in the wrong locations.
- Provide sanitation recommendations for food-service accounts.
- Food debris present within the account competes with cockroach bait placements.
- Note the presence of food debris and sanitation issues needing correction on service inspection documents. Provide the account with copies of the inspection report and written recommendations for correction of conditions.
- Learn the day-to-day operation and flow of commerce within the account. Doing so will help identify problem areas and how roaches may move due to human activities.
- Remember that cockroaches live in a three-dimensional world. Learn to *think like a cockroach* when inspecting and servicing your accounts.
- Look carefully when inspecting and servicing an account. Think, *Where would the roaches hide in this area?* and consider what is above, below, and adjacent to the area.
- Remember that cockroaches prefer warm, humid, and undisturbed areas to harbor.
- Be sure you are properly equipped to handle the job before you arrive.
- Remember that food-service areas are often washed down every day. Residual insecticides may be removed within minutes of your work. As such, choose application locations carefully so you are not wasting your time and resources.
- Everything happens for a reason. When roaches are a persistent problem at an account, re-inspect and ask questions to learn why. None of us knows all the answers all the time, and sometimes it's best to ask a colleague for a second opinion to resolve a problematic situation.
- Treat account locations one section at a time. Dividing large account locations into sections tends to make the work easier and more manageable.
- When a large number of cockroaches are found, there is a good chance there may be additional pockets of infestation that is more widespread than first believed.

THE COCKROACH COMBAT MANUAL II

- Look beyond the aggregation for additional pockets of roaches. Treat the main pocket last.
- Stock rotation is important in cockroach control. Inspect storage areas where stock has been present an extended period of time. Look especially in areas where cardboard boxes of foodstuffs are stored. Roaches often set up housekeeping in cardboard boxes.
- Mops, brooms, and other items where food debris may be present can become infested.
- It may be necessary to drill holes to provide injection points for treatment of hidden wall voids and other such areas where roaches may harbor.
- Poor sanitation and convoluted construction are no excuse for failed cockroach control. Remember, the customer is paying the pest professional to resolve the cockroach problem. It may take longer in some accounts, but it is possible to eliminate cockroaches, provided the necessary work is completed.
- We're humans and maybe not as experienced as the cockroach. Remember, cockroaches have been successful on the planet for more than three hundred and fifty million years and may have been in some accounts for ten or more years. Such infestations may not be successfully resolved in just one or a few service visits and follow-up work is often necessary.
- When inspecting for cockroaches if the light is off when you enter a room, leave it off. Inspect with your flashlight and then turn the lights on and observe where the roaches run. They'll tell you where they're hiding if you let them.
- Get to know the people who work at the account and learn who the key person is (the one who turns on the lights in the morning). Talk to that person. He or she will be the one who likely knows where the cockroaches are seen and where they hide.
- Roaches come from roaches. If you leave some behind, their population will likely rebound over time.
- Roaches can reproduce quickly, so there is no such thing as a minor infestation.
- Be proud of the work you do. Cockroaches can spread various pathogens and cause illnesses to innocent consumers of the food you're there to protect.
- The job is not complete until the paperwork is done. Keep well documented, complete, and legible service records.

Schools

Years ago when working in New York on Long Island, the state introduced an "IPM in schools" program that required certain methodologies and criteria. Some viewed this program to mean pesticide free, but that viewpoint was somewhat narrow and incorrect. During this time a cockroach infestation occurred at an elementary school within a large school system. German cockroaches were discovered in a first-grade classroom and in the cafeteria kitchen.

CHAPTER 11: SPECIAL SITUATIONS

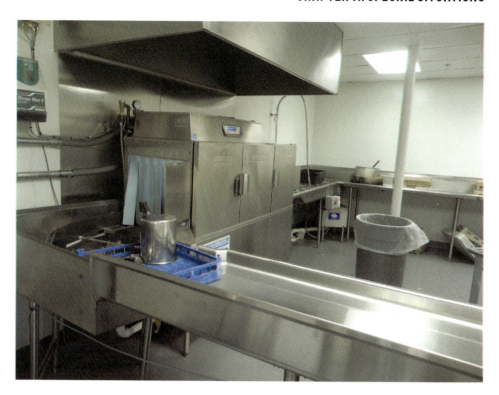

PHOTO 11.5: **Schools include kitchen facilities that rival commercial kitchen accounts. With many meals served each day, school kitchens are under continued threat of cockroach infestation.**

When fielding the call from the district superintendent to discuss the situation, a memorable comment was made and for good reason. This superintendent had previous experience with a significant cockroach infestation and was understandably concerned that another such event was occurring.

The conversation touched on IPM, to which the superintendent responded (I'm paraphrasing here), "Look, I don't care about that IPM crap, you get down here as soon as possible and nuke this entire place. I want no roaches here by Monday morning, and I don't care what you have to do, just do it."

At that time my observation was that IPM is a good thing; however, when people are motivated by certain factors, they seem to want their cockroaches eliminated no matter what by whatever means.

Following are practical tips relative to cockroach control in restaurant and food-handling facilities for your review and consideration.

- Many states have or are in the process of adopting certain pest-management regulations for schools, daycare facilities, and similar accounts.
- Do not apply pesticide products in the presence of school children.
- Proper documentation of service work is required. Be sure to include the name of the product applied, the quantity, the site/location of application, and the time.
- Avoid incurring avoidable liabilities as a pest professional. Assure that all service technicians are well-trained and suitably aware of local regulations regarding pest-management procedures in schools, daycare facilities, and similar accounts.

- Children may have allergies to various materials. Consider this when choosing certain products, materials, and supplies.
- Keep all pesticides and control devices out of reach of children.
- Know the normal hours of operation of the account and make arrangements to conduct pest-management services outside the hours when children will be present.
- Consider the implementation of least-toxic solutions for use at these accounts.
- When pesticides must be used to resolve a cockroach infestation, do so during the hours when no students are present.
- Provide written recommendations for pest prevention that will enhance your professional pest-management efforts.
- Complete well-documented inspection and service reports and supply copies of these reports to the account administrator.
- Some school locations may be interested in holding "bug classes" to educate their students.
- Ensure that your liability insurance provides proper coverage and completed operations coverage for professional services conducted at the type of accounts being serviced.

Zoos and Animal Facilities

Cockroaches and other pests are commonly encountered at zoos and animal facilities. These locations include various environments that are intended to house live animals and are capable of providing all the needed resources for cockroach populations to thrive. Of course the challenge that must be overcome by pest professionals is figuring out how to eliminate the cockroaches without harming the animal residents. Plus, there are other factors that must be considered: dealing with veterinarians; animal psychologists; maintaining the aesthetics; working behind the scenes; restrictions on product use; the diversity of the animals present; and animals may consume dead roaches all serve to complicate the cockroach control work.

When working at an animal research facility, a variety of primates was present. This facility conducted research on serious communicable diseases. Working where large primates such as chimpanzees are present is problematic. Basically, these are wild animals, and even though they may be assimilated to their caretakers, they don't take kindly to strangers. It is wise to heed the warnings of the staff and to remember that these are wild animals that possess amazing strength and little regard for human life—not a good combination.

One animal handler warned to keep far from the cage, because if a chimp was able to grab you, he'd try to pull you through the bars, resulting in slow and painful injuries. In addition, these large primates entertain themselves by *throwing*. This means they pick up their feces and throw it at unwary individuals. In fact, staff rigged a clothes rack with Plexiglas that could be used as a rolling shield when walking along the row of enclosures. Thankfully it worked.

Cockroaches are immune to the throwing and not encumbered by the cages nor the presence of locked doors. No, the roaches have the run of such places and can quickly build significant populations beyond the bars, within the animal habitats, and throughout the facility. The diversity of animals present presents additional challenges. Some animals will feed on dead roaches, some animals are large, some are small; and others may be adversely affected by pesticides. Others may be housed in glass cages that are completely exposed to public view, while others live in uniquely designed habitats that cannot be serviced in such a way that the aesthetics would not be affected.

A glass enclosure was exposed to public view on three sides. It contained burrows, foliage, and hollow tree trunks in which the animals would roam, and these areas were infested with American cockroaches. The solution here was the design of durable stations that would only allow the roaches to enter while being strong enough to withstand destruction efforts of the animals and blend with the aesthetics of the enclosure.

PHOTO 11.6: **Animal enclosures provide natural environments that include unlimited food, moisture, and harborage resources for cockroaches in combination with significant challenges that must be considered and overcome by pest professionals.**

Following are practical tips relative to cockroach control in zoo and animal facilities for your review and consideration.

- It can be challenging to deal with certain animal specialists, and the experienced pest professionals know to be considerate of concerns of these individuals who primarily intend to protect the safety and well-being of their animals.
- Animal caretakers are keen on non-toxic and least toxic solutions for use in animal enclosures. Solutions and methodologies such as vacuums are well received options.
- Logistical challenges due to the presence of live animals may call for creativity beyond the norm for pest professionals.

- Viewable animal enclosures cannot be baited for cockroaches in the same fashion as a kitchen cabinet. Any bait placement may not be in view of the public and must be inaccessible to the animal displayed yet accessible to the target cockroaches. The result is an animal-proof bait enclosure that roaches can enter and feed within and is inaccessible and indestructible to the animal present as well.
- Provide written recommendations for zoo and animal facility staff that will enhance the cockroach-control efforts.
- Sanitation is a constant concern of cockroach control. Excess food as well as feces can serve as a food resource for cockroaches.
- Use sticky traps with caution in such facilities due to risk of inadvertently catching an animal. Sticky traps should be placed in areas inaccessible to the animals. Place monitor traps outside the animal enclosure. They may also be placed within pipes to protect the animals from the glue trap.

Transportation

The cockroach is no stranger to various modes of transportation. In fact, cockroach pests are thought to have been dispersed throughout the world having traveled with man in ships. It is not uncommon for a pest professional to be called about roaches on a commercial airline, bus, train, truck, or other type of vehicle. Some significant cockroach infestations have been on ships.

City and long-haul buses commonly have cockroach problems. The backseats can be problematic for a variety of reasons. People change baby diapers on the backseat, food debris may be present due to passengers eating, the seats located over the wheel wells trap debris, which attracts cockroaches, and the driver's seat area may have roaches due to the driver's consumption of snacks and other foods there.

Commercial airlines serve food, allow passengers to bring food onboard, and provide little downtime for pest management services to be performed. These planes travel to multiple climates where roaches may wander onboard. With each flight the plane takes on additional food and beverages. Airplanes contain sophisticated electronics and circuit boards, which may be harmed by traditional pesticide application. Additionally, the plane is a relatively small enclosed space where pesticide residues and odors may be problematic and cause for concern.

- Passengers may stuff food debris and wrappers into the seat pockets, making them more difficult to clean, which favors the cockroach.
- Planes are not cleaned with the same frequency as they used to be. These reduced cleaning schedules favor the cockroach.
- Airplanes contain sophisticated electronics. Care must be taken to avoid any application or pest-management methodologies that may compromise electronic components.

CHAPTER 11: SPECIAL SITUATIONS

- Planes travel great distances and from diverse locations, bringing exotic and unfamiliar pest species with them. Be on the lookout, and don't be surprised by such foreign pests.
- Monitors, physical removal, and bait placements may be well-suited for use on airplanes.
- Speak to cleaning crews and service personnel to gain insights as to pest sightings when servicing planes.
- Avoid using odorous products, as airplanes are basically enclosed flying tubes with little if any air circulation.

Prisons

Pest management in prisons can be difficult and dangerous work. The detainees can be dangerous. There may be restrictions as to what products and equipment are allowed for use within the prison and when the work may be done. In a similar fashion to servicing a school, prisoners may not be present during normal pest-management service work, and service work may need to be scheduled during certain times that are dictated to the pest professional.

Here are some comments and tips for your review and consideration when working within prisons.

- Be aware and considerate of the environment you're working in and the people you encounter.
- Be sure to have a photo identification badge when working in secure environments and locations.
- Understand the various limitations and restrictions when working in prisons.
- Get to know the key contact people at the prison locations where you're working and be sure they know you. It could save your life one day.
- Be aware that some detainees may be sensitive to various pest-management devices and procedures. Some may be offended by the presence of sticky traps because the trapped animal may be viewed as a prisoner itself.

Chapter 12

Solving Cockroach Problems

Any pest professional who has been working cockroach-infested accounts for any length of time has had at least one account where the cockroaches seemingly can't be controlled. Even despite the numerous visits, your best efforts, and countless man hours, the roaches persist, leaving us to wonder, *How can this be? What's happening? What should be done?* Assuredly, no pest technician wants to be defeated by a cockroach situation at any account.

However, when faced with a seemingly uncontrollable or unsolvable cockroach situation, what's needed is a viable solution that may exist just beyond our grasp. The question is; *how can the technician attain this solution when working in the field?*

Generally speaking, a systematic approach that incorporates various perspectives and viable methodologies is a successful problem-solving technique. Discussing the situation and seeking the perspective and advice of other professionals is helpful.

Doing the same thing over and over and expecting different results has been called the definition of insanity. If what you're doing at an account is not working, it is likely time to change what you're doing. Following are various cockroach problem-solving tips and photos for your review and consideration.

PHOTO 12.1: **Don't overlook floor drains and sewer lines, which can be the source of cockroach problems. These can be cleaned with steam and baited.**

- It may not be the product you're applying but where and how the product is being applied.
- Learn what happens in the areas you inspect and treat after you leave. Assume your applications may be subjected to cleaning or other work that may affect long-term efficacy.
- Learn the names of the people who work at the account and their respective roles. Those folks who work the early and late shifts are likely the best *eyes and ears on the ground* to assist you in learning where the roaches are most sighted. These folks can be a wealth of information to the pest professionals who takes the time to utilize this valuable resource.
- Cockroaches are predictable. We know their preferences. Think of these preferences when searching for persistent pockets of roach populations at problem accounts.

PHOTO 12.2: **It is difficult to gain control in residences where clutter and food debris are present. Be sure to document this and communicate this to your account management.**

- It has been said: *Sometimes we may be too close to the trees to see the forest.* Back off and view the account from afar so you can the potential harborage areas that roaches may utilize that may have averted previous detection.
- Doc has told us for years: "Learn to think like a roach." Think about where you would hide if you were a cockroach.
- Sanitation and food debris can be difficult to overcome at some account locations. Be sure to document the presence of food debris, unsatisfactory sanitary conditions and suitable recommendations in service reports. Be sure to communicate this information to the client.

PHOTO 12.3: **Cockroaches may feed on your rodent bait creating additional problems.**

- These days, digital cameras are inexpensive. Photos are an excellent tool for communicating the presence of sanitation and other concerns that need to be addressed.
- Be sure to have a pest-sighting log in place and rely on the information therein to help you when investigating a cockroach problem at the account.
- Think like Sherlock Holmes: explore all the possibilities and the evidence present.
- Be sure to correctly identify the cockroach prior to implementing control procedures.
- Nothing happens in a vacuum. There are always reasons cockroaches may be present at the account. Your job is to figure out why and then provide solutions.

PHOTOS 12.4 AND 12.5: **It is necessary to remove drawers and get on your knees to be able to see these cockroaches hiding under countertops and in cabinets.**

- Remember that roaches such as American cockroaches may travel great distances. The source harborage may be far from where you are searching.
- Use monitor traps to your advantage when investigating an ongoing problem at an account.
- Keep a well-documented log of pertinent information that you may refer to in the event of a subsequent problem at an account.
- Note that poor handwriting will become a problem in the future when you may need to refer to previous service reports. Writing quickly but illegibly will ultimately cost you time and not save time.
- Think about what is possible.
- German cockroaches prefer warm areas with elevated humidity. Such areas as refrigeration and appliance motors, water heaters, and other such equipment fixtures may provide suitable but hidden harborage areas that may have been overlooked in previous services.

PHOTO 12.6: In apartments, the water heater is sometimes hidden under the countertop in the corner, where access to this warm, humid area preferred by cockroaches is blocked by either the range, dishwasher, or cabinetry.

- Various types of equipment present at the infested account may require the use of suitable hand tools to open and access for inspection and service.
- When an area is inaccessible for inspection and service at an account, note this in your service report. Place monitors in suitable locations around the perimeter of such areas so that the presence of roaches coming from this areas may be documented.
- When accessibility to a potentially infested area is a concern, send a written request for service access to the area and follow up.
- At hospitality locations, hospitality and maintenance department staff are a good source of knowledge and assistance for cockroach control.
- Note that service carts can transport roaches. Be sure to include the inspection of such carts in your cockroach-serviced protocol.

THE COCKROACH COMBAT MANUAL II

PHOTO 12.7: **To conduct a thorough cockroach inspection, it is necessary to open all cabinets, remove all drawers, and check areas where cockroaches may harbor.**

- A coffee, vending, or ice machine can harbor cockroaches, so don't overlook them.
- Account employees who store foodstuffs at their desks can become a source of a persistent cockroach problem. Be sure to address this issue in your investigation as well as in written recommendations for the account staff.
- Utility penetrations and chases may serve to allow roaches to travel from room to room and across various areas. Be sure to adequately inspect and include such areas in your investigation.
- Confirm your suspicions using sticky traps.
- Even a water fountain can harbor cockroaches.
- Do not overlook elevator shafts, pits, and motor rooms.
- Escalator pits and motors may be problematic and require inspection and service.

PHOTO 12.8: **American cockroaches can travel great distances from preferred areas such as warm steam tunnels and utility chases, where hot pipes provide them suitable hidden habitat.**

- Electronic control and computer rooms may be locked and difficult to access. Document accessibility issues, communicate accessibility requests in writing, and don't take no for an answer when warranted. Remind the client that the roaches don't have any such accessibility restrictions.
- Consider what has changed at the account that may be responsible for or related to the existing cockroach problem. Has a recent delivery arrived? Have they changed vendors?

Pest management is extremely interesting work, especially when a professional viewpoint as a forensic entomologist is adopted.

Chapter 13

Frequently-Asked Questions

What species of cockroach is the largest?
The Giant Cockroach, *Blaberus giganteus*, of Central America, is the largest cockroach in the world. Adult males and females are about three inches and four inches long, respectively.

What species of cockroach is the fastest?
The American cockroach, *Periplaneta americana*, is probably the fastest cockroach. However, there are other roach species that are also very fast such as the Turkistan roach.

How many species of cockroaches are there?
There are about four thousand cockroach species worldwide. However, only a few are considered structural pests.

How long can a cockroach live without food?
The larger species, such as American, Australian, smokey brown, and Oriental, can live about one month without food. German cockroaches can only make it about two weeks.

How long can a cockroach live without water?
A cockroach can live about two weeks without water.

Can a cockroach really live without its head?
The cockroach body can remain alive for about a week without its head. However, is this actually living? There is no feeding going on even though the body may be moving or reacting via reflex.

How fast can cockroach run?
Researchers have clocked American cockroaches at more than three miles per hour. When scaled to a six-foot man, this would be equivalent to the man being able to run more than 170 mph.

Which species of cockroach is the top pest?
There are only a few cockroach species that are actually structural pests. The German cockroach is likely the number-one roach pest, with the American cockroach close behind.

Are water bugs really cockroaches?
The term water bug has been used to describe a number of insect pests in and around a home. American, Oriental, Smokey brown, and other roach species are all referred to as water bugs. A true water bug belongs to the order Hemiptera. They are adapted for aquatic life. These are aquatic insects that feed on aquatic life such as insects, small fish, and amphibians.

What is a palmetto bug?
A palmetto bug is usually an American cockroach. However, there are some people that refer to any large cockroach, regardless of species, as a palmetto bug.

How do cockroaches climb glass?
Not all cockroaches can climb glass and other such smooth surfaces. Roaches that can climb have sticky pads, which they must keep clean, on their feet or tarsi.

Do domestic cockroaches have natural enemies?
Aside from humans, there are a number of other pests that feed on them. Mice, rats, and other cockroaches all do well attacking them. Rats and mice may run vertically up a rough basement wall to snatch live cockroaches resting on the wall. Mice are known to actually inspect sticky traps and feed on live but captured cockroaches there. This is why technicians may find just portions of cockroaches or just legs remaining on sticky traps.

When the food supply is low and the cockroach population is high, the cockroaches may feed upon each other. The newly molted cockroaches, often mistaken as albinos, are susceptible to such predation by other their fellow cockroaches. Even German cockroaches bred in laboratories can have predators. When visiting a lab in California, a stream of Argentine ants was observed entering from the outdoors and carrying away cockroach body parts. When asked what was going on, the lab staff reported that the Argentine ants were attacking all their containers. As this was problematic for the lab they had allowed the ants access to certain containers to keep them from attacking and ruining ongoing trials going on in other containers nearby.

Aside from these predators, cockroaches also have problems with fungi and internal parasites. No one cares, but they die of old age.

Why and how do cockroaches hiss?
The Madagascar hissing cockroach is noted for hissing. The hiss is a defense mechanism. These roaches quickly squeeze their upper and lower sections of their body together. Doing so forces air out of their spiracles, their breathing ports located along the side of their body, to create the hiss sound.

Is it safe to eat cockroaches?
No, not really. Cockroaches may have a large amount of bacteria on or in their bodies that could cause various illnesses.

Can I get cockroaches in my apartment from the neighboring apartment?
Yes. Cockroaches can easily spread from apartment to apartment in multifamily dwellings.

Why do I hate cockroaches so much?
Cockroaches are an insect much maligned in the public eye. We might wonder why these creatures are met with such disdain; however, many would agree it is well earned. Certainly many would agree that cockroaches are disgusting. They invade our homes and set up housekeeping in our personal space and belongings. They infest our cabinets, pantries, and storage areas where we keep our food, medicine, dishes, pots, pans, and utensils. They contaminate these areas with their fecal matter, are odorous, and can infect us with various pathogens.

How can a cockroach end up inside an ice cube in my iced tea?
It is not unheard of that cockroaches may enter an ice-maker machine. Once inside the machine it is possible the cockroach slipped into the mechanism where it became trapped in the cold water during ice formation. Next time, check your ice cubes prior to placing them in your glass.

Can people carry cockroaches on their body like they do bed bugs?
Yes. It is not common, but some people may have so many in their home or apartment that they unknowingly carry a few on their clothing when they leave. Cockroaches may be transported by man, but we don't consider them adept at hitchhiking as we do bed bugs.

How can a cockroach live in a jar for days without air?
Insects are small and require less air to survive than what appears to us. There is much more air in an average-sized jar than we think. There may be enough air for an insect such as a cockroach to survive in a jar for months. However, the more limiting factors to survival are water and food.

Cockroaches seem to be cleaning their antennae. Are they clean animals?
They do clean or preen their antennae often to remove materials so they can continue to function. However, they are not clean animals. Refer to Chapter 4 for additional information on cockroaches and diseases.

I tried to crush a cockroach with my shoe but it ran away when I lifted my foot. How is this possible?
You likely did not hit it directly or it got tucked into the space created by the heel of your shoe. No cockroach can withstand the full impact and crushing pressure of a human's shoe.

I opened my refrigerator and found cockroaches tucked inside the door. How can this happen?
As populations build, cockroaches may be forced to find additional cracks and crevices to hide in. Refrigerator and freezer doors have a gasket that is intended to seal in the

cold. However, these gaskets provide cracks and crevices in which cockroaches can harbor. Sometimes these gaskets can tear. When the torn gasket is the hollow type, cockroaches can enter and hide. Even at low temperatures above freezing, they can survive for weeks.

I've heard that only cockroaches can survive a nuclear war. Is it possible that cockroaches can survive a direct hit from an atomic bomb?
No, what can? Cockroaches can survive higher levels of radiation than most animals; however, they would not be able to survive a ground zero hit.

Do cockroaches live in sewers? How is this possible?
Yes, some species can survive quite well in sewer pipes. We need to realize that no sewer pipe is completely full even when sewage may be flowing. These pipes are likely just about half-full on average. This provides plenty of room for cockroaches to hang on to the upper portions of the pipes. American cockroaches can build huge populations or tens of thousands of roaches in numerous cities across the United States. Although rare, German cockroaches have also been seen in sewer pipes in Curacao. This may have been because it is dry there most of the year and the environment within these pipes provides much-needed moisture.

How do cockroaches know where to hide?
Initially, the cockroaches are opportunistic and head for the first protective area. If suitable, they smear that spot with their fecal matter. The fecal matter contains pheromones that attract other cockroaches, and these areas are known as fecal focal points. The scent helps the cockroach return to the same areas, and the more the roaches frequent these areas, the more cockroaches will harbor there. Cockroach antennae have sensory organs that help it detect or pick up the smell. German cockroaches can detect these scents from up to about ten feet. Large peridomestic cockroaches such as the American and Smokey brown cockroach can hone in from about forty yards or more, depending on which way the wind is blowing.

Why are American cockroaches and other large species found on top floors of high-rise buildings? How do they get up there?
American cockroaches can travel great distances. They may start from the sewer level but access upper floors through various routes, including elevator shafts, utility chases, trash chutes, and other void areas. In the wild they climb trees and launch from heights to make it easier to fly.

What is a flying cockroach?
Most adult cockroaches have wings and are capable of flight or gliding. German cockroaches have wings but cannot fly. The warmer and more humid an area is, the more likely cockroaches are to fly. American cockroaches readily fly in the South. In the north they do not; however, in steam tunnels they can and do, even in northern locations.

Are cockroaches attracted to lights at night?
Some, including the Asian and adult male wood cockroaches, are. You can reduce the chance of these cockroaches entering your home by limiting exterior lighting.

Can you ever seal every crack and crevice cockroaches enter?
No. Electric appliances, motors, drawers, and other such areas cannot easily be sealed. However, the space around and adjacent to moldings, pipe, utility penetrations, and cracks in walls can be sealed. These are important areas to seal to help reduce cockroach populations.

Do ultrasonic sound devices repel cockroaches?
No. There is no published data from any credible source that proves that these devices actually work. However, many of these units are sold each year to people who hope they work.

Do electromagnetic devices repel cockroaches?
No. And cockroaches may even live within them and do very well.

I once tried to kill cockroaches in a microwave oven. Why didn't it work?
Microwaves can kill cockroaches. However, the roaches may move to the corners and edges within the microwave unit to avoid exposure to the microwaves.

Why are sticky trap monitors so important to use in every account?
We can't be in every account every day. Sticky traps work for us 24/7 and are cost-effective. They help us make early detection of a problem as well as help identify problem areas.

How long should sticky monitors be out before a good indication of activity is achieved?
Usually an adequate indication is attained within twenty-four hours, and you will know if there are any cockroaches within the area. Beyond that, the numbers trapped will continue to build. If numbers are very low to begin with, it may take two or three days before any become trapped.

What can a homeowner or apartment resident do to minimize the chance of getting cockroaches, and what can they do if they get a problem?
Check boxes, packages, and bags of items brought in from outside sources. Keep sticky traps in critical areas (refer to information on trap placement elsewhere in this book), and check them daily or as often as possible. Keep a tight lid on garbage containers, especially at night. Limit the amount of clutter in your home. Store food materials in sealed plastic bags or tightly covered containers. Once in a while after dark, turn on the lights to see if any cockroaches are present.

What should you do when you see even one cockroach?
Check hidden areas for more. Place additional sticky traps. Call for professional pest-management service or place cockroach baits as per label directions. If your building has

a contract with a pest-management professional, call the management office to schedule an inspection and service.

If German cockroaches can multiply so quickly and develop resistance to current control products, how are we going to contain them in the future?
Fortunately, cockroaches are such an important pest that researchers are continually working to find new solutions. Researchers at global basic manufacturers such as Bayer, BASF, FMC, MGK, Nisus, Syngenta, and others are always seeking the next cockroach silver bullet.

How does "going green" favor the survival of cockroaches?
We believe trying to be environmentally responsible is a good thing, and we can't argue with this concept. It also gives you an example of how adaptive cockroaches can become.

Examples of how cockroaches have benefited from our good environmental intentions include

- No longer incinerating trash to avoid air pollution. This trash accumulates at landfills, and these areas serve as a tremendous breeding grounds that are difficult to access to provide control.
- Recycling all sorts of bottles, newspapers, cardboard, and other such items. These recyclables create clutter, harborage, and food resource for cockroaches.
- Biodegradable packaging materials that are often made from starch-like materials. Cockroaches can feed on these materials. Suddenly the mail room or shipping department at an office building can be a hot spot for cockroaches.

How do I know if I purchase something it will work?
Before you purchase a product or insecticide for cockroach control, find out which independent research facility documented that it works, how long it's been available on the market, and who else is using the product. Written testimonials offer little if any value.

Why do cockroaches group together?
In the research laboratory we have been able to show that when cockroaches are isolated in individual chambers, the rate of survival is lower, and the time required to reach adulthood is longer. The benefits of group living can only be speculated on. However, it is suggested that by living in groups, cockroaches create a microenvironment with increased humidity that provides mutual benefits that enhance their survival.

Is it possible for me to get rid of cockroaches in an apartment if my neighbors have them?
Yes and no. Yes, if your neighbors cooperate and allow all apartments to be treated properly. No, if at least one neighbor does nothing and allows the cockroaches to breed and serves as a reservoir population that may travel via various utility lines and other such routes to infest neighboring units. It is possible, however, to provide reasonable control in some apartments if suitable management methodologies are implemented.

What can I do to decrease the number of cockroaches coming from my neighbor?
Proofing can be done by stuffing copper wool, caulk, and other such materials into various openings that cockroaches may use as access and entry points. Such openings around utility penetrations, floor moldings, and other such areas should be sealed. Sealers such as caulk, Xcluder, and other such materials may be used. Additionally, it is wise to try to get neighbors to cooperate with the pest-management professionals contracted by the apartment management if such service exists.

Is the presence of cockroaches in my place a sign of poor housekeeping?
No. A few cockroaches may be brought in or enter the cleanest of homes undetected at any time. However, their build up and increased population occurs as a result of neglecting the problem.

Is it ever possible to get rid of cockroaches completely from a home?
Yes, and competent professionals do this on a daily basis. However, you may have a re-infestation if you live in an area where risk of infestation is high due to local conditions. If you're having a cockroach problem, it is wise to rely on the services of experienced pest-management professionals.

What are cockroach droppings?
Cockroach droppings are their fecal matter. They plaster it on wood or cardboard surfaces, usually in hidden areas where they harbor or hide. In areas where the fecal matter does not stick, it will drop to the nearest surface. The scientific analysis of such fecal matter is called scatology. Each cockroach species produces a uniquely shaped and sized fecal pellet.

How smart are cockroaches? Do they have brains?
Cockroaches do not have brains in the normal sense as humans have and understand what a brain is. They have a concentration of nerves in their heads that serve as a focal point for their nervous system. Cockroaches can learn from experience how to travel a maze. They have enough sense to avoid some pesticide-treated surfaces and move rapidly from extremely hot, dry, or cold areas. This creature has been able to survive for more than three hundred and fifty million years, and despite man's best efforts to eradicate it, it continues to thrive. Biologists view the survival instincts of the cockroach with high regard.

Can cockroaches eat toothpaste or soap?
Cockroaches will eat both toothpaste and soap. We don't know if they can digest soap. We do know mice can consume bar soap, likely for the fat content therein.

I left a half-filled cup of coffee on the kitchen counter. The following morning there was a dead cockroach in it. How did it get there?
The cockroach's antennae were able to detect the odor and moisture emitted from the coffee within the cup. The cockroach then climbed into the cup to feed and failed to get a

good foothold. Basically it fell in, could not get out, and eventually drowned. Cockroaches can swim but may eventually expire because they need to be able to pull themselves up onto "dry land."

What good are cockroaches?
Cockroaches are natural scavengers and help consume, recycle, and clean up waste materials. However, the domestic pest species currently serve no known beneficial purpose.

What do I do if my guest arrives and a cockroach appears?
You can do a number of things. Don't spray any pesticides because you may flush additional cockroaches out while also having to deal with the pesticide odor. Leave the lights on because cockroaches prefer to stay in the dark. Stifle yourself, don't tell your guests, and call for professional pest-management services the next day.

What is insect phobia?
Insect phobia is an exaggerated fear of the presence of insects when none actually exist. These phobic individuals will go as far to develop rashes, lose sleep, present bite symptoms, and come close to a nervous breakdown. Many times the cause of such circumstances are not due to insects at all, and there may be other factors that come into play, including fabric, laundry detergent, allergies, new materials within the home such as curtains or carpeting, jewelry, and other such things.

Can cockroaches bite me?
Cockroaches have chewing mouthparts, so technically speaking, yes, they can bite. However, the damage a cockroach may or may not be able to inflict upon a human through biting alone is minimal due to the size of its mouthparts. A large population of large cockroaches, such as American cockroaches, may be able to do some harm, but this would be an extreme case.

In a case where a victim was allegedly abused cockroach biting/chewing was suspected. To determine this we forced exposed, starved American cockroaches to the abdominal skin tissue of a colleague (a forensic entomologist) for about thirty minutes to determine if these cockroaches would bite, feed, and/or cause harm to humans. Not only could he feel the cockroaches biting him, those American cockroaches readily bit, fed, and left scars. In our observation, the scaring appeared as abrasions to the skin, but there was no bleeding. It matched the scars on the abused victim.

What are the control methods of the future?
We look to a pest-management approach where sanitation and the elimination of favorable cockroach harborages will play a major role in management, and pesticides will take a minor role. We also look forward to chemical formulations that will interfere with the roaches' prolific reproductive abilities.

What purpose do the odors of cockroaches serve?
There is a distinct variation in the odor of different cockroach species. A good cockroach technician can walk into an infested apartment, take a good whiff, and, if there is a heavy population present, be able to tell the species present. These odors serve sexual purposes and encourage pocketing or aggregation of cockroach populations.

How long do cockroaches live?
German cockroaches can live about a year under ideal field conditions. American and Oriental cockroaches can survive about two years or longer.

What is the difference between licensing and certification for pest management professionals?
A pest-control operator can obtain a license by paying a fee, so having a license is no assurance or indication that he is necessarily qualified. Certification, however, requires that the pest-management professional has taken and passed an exam that indicates a level of knowledge and competence.

Do certain types of restaurants have more cockroaches than other types?
No, the cuisine or type of restaurant has nothing to do with cockroach infestation levels. Caring restaurant managers keep a clean and tidy restaurant and are aware of pest-management needs. Careless managers, regardless of restaurant type, will encourage cockroach infestations and resulting populations to build through their lack of attention to pest-management practices and corrective action needs.

Are certain restaurants more likely to have cockroaches?
Yes. Restaurants that do not have professional pest-management services, that have employees with cockroaches in their own homes, that take deliveries from suppliers who have infested warehouses, and that are basically unaware of pest-management fundamentals are more likely to have cockroach and other pest problems.

Don't only dirty homes have cockroaches?
Not necessarily. People who keep dirty homes may be poor housekeepers and tend to do little when they find cockroaches. Therefore, the cockroach problem persists and grows. Initially, cockroaches are not prejudiced and will enter and infest any home. Anyone can get cockroaches. It's no disgrace to get cockroaches, but it's a disgrace to keep them.

Why haven't cockroaches developed resistance to boric acid?
Cockroaches have shown to develop resistance after exposure to various organic synthetic insecticides over many generations. These insects develop biochemical pathways to detoxify or neutralize pesticides. Boric acid is not an organic synthetic insecticide. It works on several different systems of the cockroach, thereby making resistance to it more difficult to develop. Boric acid is a stomach poison and contact poison.

CHAPTER 13: FREQUENTLY-ASKED QUESTIONS

What should I do when I see a cockroach while dining in a restaurant?

Pest professionals are different from normal folks. Our eyes are constantly scanning for pest movement. It is not uncommon for us to be out enjoying a meal and see a cockroach crawling up a wall. If you see a cockroach in a food-service establishment, alert your server and ask to speak to the manager. Remind him to contact his pest-management professional and of the health hazards cockroach infestation poses to the public. No matter what you decide to do, if this should happen to you while dining, be sure to at least say something. Remember, cockroaches can spread disease to people.

My pest professional tells me not to do anything that would affect the efficacy of his cockroach treatment. Why does he say this?

Your pest professional has good reason for telling you this. When cockroach baits are being used, we want to avoid using insecticides that may cause the bait to become unpalatable to the roaches, and we want to avoid using baits treated with insecticides that may be repellent to roaches. Application of repellent insecticides may affect the efficacy of non-repellent insecticides applied by your professional as well. Additionally, we need to avoid disturbing monitor trap placements.

What products can I purchase that actually work to kill cockroaches in my home?

It is not as important which product is applied as much as how that product is applied. There are retail products that contain the same active ingredients that the professionals use. However, when applied in a manner inconsistent with the label language, applied in an incorrect fashion, or applied in the wrong locations, even the best cockroach products will not work as well as they should.

Are sticky traps a good thing to use?

Yes. Sticky traps are a useful tool for detecting and indicating areas of cockroach infestation. An experienced pest professional knows how to read a sticky trap to determine the extent of a cockroach infestation and other factors related to cockroaches at an account.

Are baits for cockroaches a good thing to use?

Yes. Cockroach baits are nothing new, but the baits available now are far superior to ones that were available many years ago. Today's baits may kill the roach that originally fed on it as well as other roaches.

Appendix I:
"Classic Frishman"

Over the years, Dr. Austin M. Frishman has published numerous columns and articles that have appeared in *Pest Control* and *Pest Management Professional* magazines. He has been a sought-after speaker who has presented to thousands of pest-management professionals across the United States and abroad. In his many published works, the pest-management industry has benefited from his willingness to share his observations and unique perspective. Those lucky enough to attend his presentations have received countless pages of his articles and handouts.

PHOTO 13.1: **As a popular featured speaker, Dr. Austin M. Frishman presents at an industry conference. Countless pest industry professionals have met Doc at these meetings. This is "Classic Frishman."**

We are proud to present select publications written by Dr. Austin M. Frishman. This compilation of articles and columns are "Classic Frishman," but we cannot possibly include all his written works. Others are available for review at www.pest-consultant.com.

"Classic Frishman" Titles

- "The Top 100 Best Cockroach Control Tips"
- "Typical Pests Found in and around Health-Care Facilities"
- "Twenty-Five Key Points in Writing Pest-Control Contracts for Health-Care Facilities"
- "Domestic Cockroaches and Human Bacterial Diseases"
- "Twelve Ways to Read a Sticky Trap"
- "Are Baits the Silver Bullet of Cockroach Control?"
- "Are You Using Sticky Traps the Right Way?"
- "The American Roach—High-Rise Headache"
- "How to Improve Cockroach Bait Application"
- "Questions to Ask before Treating an Office Building"
- "Death, Taxes, and Cockroach Infestations"
- "Control from the Cockroach's Perspective"

The Top 100 Best Cockroach Control Tips (for Professionals)
Dr. Austin M. Frishman

1. Care!
2. Obtain as much information as possible before starting to help you understand the account.
3. Risks of leaving cockroaches behind are higher than in the past.
4. Think like a cockroach.
5. Large space treatments, or ULVing, never worked and never will.
6. Mini ULVing an object in a plastic bag can be effective, or pop a bait station or two in the bag and leave it for a week.
7. Ninety-five percent of the work is to eliminate the last 5 percent of the cockroaches.
8. Have simple maps or diagrams of your account.
9. Whatever you did, if you double the service but do it again, it will not work if it did not work the first time.
10. Caulking has a positive impact, but it is not enough.
11. Removing shelter is the single most important item to reduce carrying capacity.
12. Large plastic bags effectively reduce harborage.
13. Large dark plastic bags in the sun can serve as a heat chamber.
14. Use sticky traps if you want to know how well you did, once you think you have control.
15. Change sticky traps as needed.
16. Do not rely on monitors alone.
17. Respond with extra action if you find even one cockroach in a sticky trap. Learn to read a sticky trap.
18. On new infestations, determine when, where, and *why* it happened.
19. Communication with the customer is critical.
20. Obtain keys to *all* locked areas.
21. Find out who the first person in the morning is who turns on the lights. Learn who has the keys to what and where they keep them.
22. Record where you place your sticky traps. Date the sticky trap when initially installed so you know how long the (zone) is pest-free.
23. Install sticky traps at different heights.
24. Encourage the client to take care of the most critical items first.
25. "Bait-mania" is not the complete answer.
26. Do not rely on customer sightings alone.
27. A strong flashlight, knee pads, and determination are critical to finding cockroaches.
28. Use an extended mirror to help inspect an area impossible to stick your head into.
29. Learn the flow pattern of as many items as possible (e.g., toilet paper, bulbs, etc.).
30. Think "3D" when hunting.
31. Bend low—really low.
32. If the population of German cockroaches is very high, start by vacuuming.

33. Use a vacuum cleaner with a HEPA-filter rated bag.
34. With high cockroach population, initially use gels before bait stations.
35. Date bait stations with an Avery dot or permanent marker.
36. You must install cockroach bait within the zone to be effective.
37. You must have the bait between where the cockroaches harbor and where they feed to achieve adequate control (elimination).
38. Installing bait stations on black baseboards in a commercial account is not a good idea. Employees will "mop" them away.
39. If theft of bait stations is a problem, consider coating the top surface with Vaseline.
40. Bait trays go in corners and against edges. An inch away can reduce effectiveness.
41. Use a long stick to help retrieve monitors or to initially place them.
42. With gels, do not fill the crack for German cockroaches.
43. With gels for the peridomestic cockroaches, do not apply in small cracks.
44. Use a wire with a paper towel or sponge to help dab gel in hard-to-reach areas.
45. Wear a headband flashlight to keep both hands free when inspecting and baiting.
46. A footstool carrying case helps make short people tall.
47. Hercules Putty helps anchor bait stations on vertical or rough surfaces.
48. Clean the surface before installing a bait tray. Use a roughened cleaning item to do so.
49. Carry a wiping cloth when applying gel.
50. Avoid gel on surfaces that reach 130 degrees F and higher.
51. Wear protective, impervious gloves when applying gel bait and when inspecting for cockroaches.
52. In areas with strong air movement, minimize gel exposure by applying gel into protected areas or devices.
53. In very dusty or dirty areas, protect cockroach bait trays and gel by inserting into folded cardboard. Place in accessible areas.
54. Protect bait stations from parrots and monkeys (when servicing animal-based locations).
55. History repeats itself. Record where you found cockroaches and when. Check these records from time to time.
56. Look for new items that were installed since your previous visit (e.g., paintings in a restaurant dining area).
57. Keep the lights off before entering a dark room. Search with a flashlight, and then turn on the lights and see where the cockroaches run.
58. Remember, the customer is the customer no matter how disagreeable he or she may be.
59. Document areas where poor sanitation and construction faults persist. Recommend they be corrected.
60. On extremely heavy infestations, check the exterior. This includes the roof.
61. In wall voids that are inaccessible, drill and dust once.
62. In extremely difficult situations, use growth regulators in inaccessible areas.

63. Ask for help if you need it. The longer you wait, the more expensive it is for your firm to correct the situation.
64. When scheduling how often to service and the amount of time to do so in a give account, do not give even time to each area. Spend more time and frequency where it is needed.
65. Once the account is pest-free, allow about 10 to 20 percent free time to roam and look for new areas on each service visit.
66. Work smarter, not harder (e.g., ask early for keys and a ladder).
67. Be sure you know what species you are trying to control.
68. Be assertive but polite when necessary.
69. Be mindful of bait avoidance.
70. Use enough bait.
71. Do not "spray" or crack and crevice on top of your bait.
72. Store the bait properly in the vehicle; use a sealed container.
73. Store the bait properly in the shop.
74. Do not smoke and bait.
75. Move the operation if necessary (e.g., move recycled bottles to the exterior).
76. In Minnesota, your can freeze it; in Miami, you can fry it.
77. Study edges (lines) as potential cockroach highways.
78. Cardboard goes or encase it.
79. Pick up pet food at night. Take out the trash or cover it.
80. Be neat. This includes not leaving the loose paper from the sticky traps around.
81. Carry a Leatherman and other tools to be able to inspect behind hidden areas.
82. Use food material on sticky traps to help lure American cockroaches onto the boards.
83. Carry bottled water and/or Gatorade with you to stay hydrated.
84. Get a good night's rest.
85. Eat a banana every day for the potassium.
86. Carry a business card with you at all times.
87. Wear a bump cap or hardhat.
88. *Listen* to what the customer is telling you.
89. In commercial accounts, push a stick down a floor hole. Mark the tip with a colored rag. Check in the basement and see exactly where the stick is. This will help orient you.
90. In difficult to access voids, construct access ports (e.g., "Billy buttons" or indentations made for access to suspended ceilings).
91. Every so often, have a supervisor or quality-assurance person check the account.
92. In commercial accounts, learn the names and become familiar with at least three different people.
93. When inspecting, bang a table, pop a chair. Be imaginative.
94. Wave your hands and smell with your nose when looking for cockroaches.
95. Keep accurate pesticide records that meet state requirements.
96. Keep all your materials in one place and work from that one area. In large accounts, move the work focal area to different locations as needed.

97. Before you leave a room, take one last look around to see what you may have missed.
98. Smile.
99. Get the service slip signed and collect payment if instructed to do so.
100. Remember, it is no disgrace to have cockroaches, just to keep them.
101. Learn how to read a bait station.
102. Smaller, more frequent gel placements work faster than fewer, larger ones.
103. Review this list from time to time.
104. Always give the customers more than they expect!

Typical Pests Found in and around Health-Care Facilities
(Note that some listed pests may be regional.)
By Dr. Austin M. Frishman, PhD, and Jeffrey B. Tucker
Edited by P. J. Bello

1. German cockroaches
2. American cockroaches
3. Oriental cockroaches
4. Brown-banded cockroaches
5. Smokey Brown cockroaches
6. Wood cockroaches
7. Head lice
8. Bed bugs
9. Fleas (from cats, dogs, or vertebrates)
10. Parasitic bird mites
11. Silverfish/fire brats
12. Honeybees
13. Paper wasps
14. Yellow jackets/hornets
15. Fire ants
16. Pharaoh ants
17. Houseflies
18. Drain flies
19. Cluster flies
20. Phorid flies
21. Blow flies
22. Fruit flies
23. Subterranean termites
24. Drywood termites
25. Invading pests (millipedes, ground beetles, earwigs, box-elder bugs, and clover mites)
26. Spiders
27. Stored product beetles and moths
28. Bats
29. Parasitic rodent mites
30. Ticks
31. House mice
32. Norway rats
33. Roof rats
34. Feral cats
35. Pigeons
36. Sparrows
37. Starlings

Most pest-control contracts do not include management of cats, birds, and termites. If there is such a problem, it can be handled as a special service.

25 Key Points When Writing Pest Control Contracts for Health-Care Facilities
By Dr. Austin M. Frishman, PhD, and Jeffrey B. Tucker
Edited by P. J. Bello

Require the submission of qualifications and references, including names and addresses of at least three other locations where the pest control contractor is currently doing similar work.

Indicate that the price submitted should include cost for services, materials, equipment, and labor. In some situations, additional materials may be needed. Allow some leeway for this situation.

An additional charge for mechanical devices such as glue boards or traps may be appropriate, provided there is prior approval from a responsible person within the health-care facility.

Indicate in the contract what pests are to be controlled. (See "Typical Pests Found in and around Health-Care Facilities.")

Require that all pesticide applicators should be certified, or, if permitted, working under the direct supervision of a certified applicator. It should also be specified that a new service person cannot be placed on the job within the health-care facility without first notifying that facility and providing a complete orientation to the building.

All pesticide labels and material safety data sheets (MSDS) must be submitted and approved before any pesticide can be used on the premises.

Indicate in the contract a specific job title within the health-care facility management structure to whom the pest-control people must report.

Include in the contract a schedule of all buildings, areas, and grounds to be treated, indicating the times of treatment required and the frequency. Allow some flexibility for open time and indicate a time frame in which additional or emergency help will be available in the event of a problem. Emergency service should be rendered within twenty-four hours.

Indicate in the contract that once the program is underway, the service schedule can be altered only with the consent of the health-care facility and that the total hours of service cannot be reduced under any circumstances. To properly create these specifications, you may need the assistance of a consultant. The larger the facility, the more complex the program.

In all facilities, indicate that an inspection of the premises will be required before a bid is accepted.

Indicate in the contract that the contractor should assign a pest-control supervisor to this facility. It should also be stated that the supervisor reports at least monthly to a designated person within the facility on the progress of the pest management program.

Indicate in the contract that all pest control materials and procedures must conform to all applicable local, state, and federal regulations. Additionally, specify that it is the responsibility

of the pest control contractor to maintain all required records and reports. Specify what type of insurance is required in terms of liability, workmen's compensation, care custody and control, pollution, and errors and omission and that any specific requirements of the state also be adhered to. Specify that this insurance must cover all the contractor's employees as well as the registered pest-control business. Require proof of this insurance.

Require the posting of a performance bond.

Make clear the length of the service agreement or contract. It is often preferable to have contracts that extend for two or three years. This assures a continuity of service.

Indicate the method and terms of invoicing and payment.

Require the pest control contractor to provide monthly written reports summarizing all pest-control activities during the previous month. Also require the pest control contractor to provide sanitation and building maintenance reports where they are applicable to the pest-control activity.

It should be indicated in the contract whether or not the pest-control contractor will be allowed to keep materials on the premises. If materials are allowed on the premises, indicate where they will be stored. Also insert into the contract a statement forbidding the disposal of any pesticides or their containers on the premises.

Indicate that the pest control contractor will provide all record-keeping forms. It should also be specified that a pest control log for the purpose of recording sitings and pest control activities will be maintained by the contractor. A copy of this log is to remain on the premises of the health-care facility at all times.

If, at the beginning of the contract period, a serious problem exists, you should state in the contract that you require an intensive cleanup operation and an ongoing service thereafter to prevent re-infestation.

Require that the pest-control contractor creates and submits, in writing and with appropriate maps included, the locations and numbers of all pest-control devices installed on the property. Examples of devices would include mechanical rodent control traps, glue boards, and cockroach bait stations.

Avoid mentioning specific pesticide products or methods of application that must be adhered to by the pest control contractor. Laws frequently change and pesticide labels change; therefore, there must be a degree of flexibility built into the contract to allow the contractor to adjust to new situations. If for some reason you decide you require a certain product or approach to be used, then state so clearly in your contract specifications. It should be stated, however, in every contract that a monitoring, surveillance, and reporting program must be instituted to evaluate the effectiveness of the pest-control program.

Require that the pest control contractor along with appropriate in-house personnel create a policy-and-procedures manual for the pest-control program. State in that manual that all pesticide applicators will stick to the policies and procedures contained therein.

State clearly in the contract how the pest-control contractor can or will be terminated if their work is unsatisfactory.

State that the pest-control contractor must conduct at least a yearly training session for various departments within the health-care facility. It is also a good idea to have the dietary, maintenance, and housekeeping departments attend a pest-control orientation provided by the pest-control contractor. This will establish the role of these various departments in the overall pest-control program.

Require that pest-control personnel wear identification badges.

Indicate in the contract the assistance that will be provided by the health-care facility. This should include but is not limited to the following:

- Appropriate keys for all locked areas.

- Designated contact person.

- Parking space designations.

- Location of areas where contractor may store materials when working on the premises.

- Assistance in removal of patients from areas to be treated.

- Assistance in properly preparing areas for treatment.

- Housekeeping and maintenance support to clean areas and repair structural problems conducive to pest problems

Domestic Cockroaches and Human Bacterial Disease

By Austin M. Frishman and I. Edward Alcamo*

Figure 1 — Cockroach exposed to test plate to determine if bacteria are present.

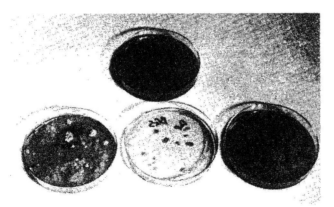

Figure 2 — Media for growth of Coliform and Salmonella. Darker dishes show presence of Salmonella.

The success several species of cockroaches have had invading the privacy of human structures is well known. Each day thousands of service technicians in the field utilize special skills to eliminate infestations of these pests. But, in the process of control, the human health problems cockroaches can manifest are often overlooked by those persons who expect instant elimination. On occasion, the importance of the health aspect may outweigh that of the nuisance aspect.

The idea that cockroaches can carry bacteria is not new. Caso first recorded this in 1898. Laboratory tests have shown that cockroaches are capable of carrying numerous disease organisms, (Jung and Schaefer, 1952, Rueger and Olsen, 1969). Cockroaches are known to carry four strains of poliomyelitis virus, about 40 species of pathogenic bacteria and the eggs of seven different species of pathogenic helminths, (Roth and Willis, 1957 and 1960). More recently, Klowden and Greenberg, 1974, showed that American cockroaches, *Periplaneta americana* (L.) are mechanical vectors of poliovirus.

The most up-to-date review on this subject, appearing in Environmental Health (Beatson, 1976), shows little field work done in this area, particularly in the United States. In January, 1976, the authors undertook a project to determine the degree that domestic cockroaches carry bacteria capable of inflicting human food poisoning and disease. The project took one year to complete.

Procedure

Live cockroaches were collected from accounts currently under ser-

---

*Professor Biology — S.U.N.Y. at Farmingdale — Entomologist.
Associate Professor, Biology — S.U.N.Y. at Farmingdale — Microbiologist.

Reprinted from Pest Control®, June, 1977, © The Harvest Publishing Company

FRISHMAN

12 ways to read sticky traps

With cockroaches on the rebound, the need to monitor with sticky traps is more important than ever. Remember that sticky traps are similar to your business cards, particularly if your company's name and telephone number are on them. Keep them clean and in unoffensive areas.

Map out where they are located. If you can't find them all to check, they are not functioning properly. Number and date when you installed each one, and keep a written record on what you find and how often you check them. This gives a picture of how long you stay pest-free, and what occurs over time.

Change the traps as needed. In some locations, it may be sufficient to leave them six months or longer. For other locations, you may need a new one every month — or sooner.

Use an Avery red dot system to mark where the traps are located in suspended ceilings. In the ceiling, place the traps in corners and by vertical columns to be the most effective.

If you find roaches on a trap but cannot find where they are coming from, install additional traps to the left and right, and/or above and below the existing trap. On the next visit, the results will help you pinpoint where they are coming from.

Install traps vertically and horizontally. Place them where they are not highly visible — they are for you to read before the client finds out he has a problem.

Here are a dozen tips on interpreting what you find:

1 No cockroaches present — This can mean there are none, or the cockroaches did not come in contact with the trap. Use a flashlight or your eyes to search.

2 Inconsistent totals — For example, your readings for four months indicate 0-0-0-40, and in the fourth month, all 40 are at different stages of development. This means that after several months of no problems, someone brought an object into the facility near the trap that has an established German cockroach population. Look for new items that came in.

3 Cockroach parts — When the trap has the legs of six cockroaches, but no bodies, mice are probably eating the cockroaches off the boards.

4 Half-eaten American cockroach adults and nymphs — Cockroaches not yet caught were able to reach over the board and feed on the struggling ones. This indicates food is a limiting factor and baits will work very well.

5 Initial counts indicate different-sized cockroaches — You have a heavy infestation.

6 Of the 20-some cockroaches on a board, 18 are on the left side — The cockroaches are moving in from the left. Search back in that direction for their harborage site.

7 You find 32 first-instar nymphs clustered on one sticky trap — This indicates an egg capsule was deposited close by. It hatched, and the young were caught on one board.

8 The trap is dusty — You have it in the wrong location, or it needs to be covered. Cockroaches cannot survive in very dusty areas.

9 The cockroaches on the board appear dead — When you blow gently over their bodies, the antennae move slowly. When you push your finger on the body, it bends. This indicates the cockroaches were caught a few days ago and are in the final stage of death.

10 Cockroaches snap at a touch. Legs and antennae fall off — These cockroaches were caught more than one week ago.

11 One or more black parasitic wasps are found on a trap — When the back end of the wasp looks cut off, you are probably looking at evaniid wasps. They parasitize the egg capsule of both American and Oriental cockroaches. For the parasites to be present, you have to have a sizeable cockroach population. They have likely been there for months to years.

12 Rodent hair is on a torn board — A mouse was caught and pulled itself off. You might say it had a bad hair day! **PC**

Dr. Austin Frishman, an industry consultant since 1967, is president of AMF Pest Management Services Inc., Boca Raton, FL. He specializes in pest management training and inspections, research and marketing, and insect and rodent strategies. Contact him at afrishman@advanstar.com.

Austin Frishman

Are Baits the Silver Bullet of Cockroach Control?

Baits are quickly becoming the tool of choice for many PCOs.

BY DR. AUSTIN FRISHMAN

A series of circumstances usually has to occur before there is a major shift in how business is done. Such is the case with baiting for cockroaches.

Today, there is little question that baiting has taken the industry by storm. The rate at which pest control companies are incorporating baiting programs as their primary method of control is noticeably high. Those who initially use baiting as a supplemental tool soon find the technicians pushing the boss for more baiting programs. Why? I believe there are some primary events that have taken place since 1980 that have propelled baits into the forefront.

Bait technology has arrived. Baits and bait applicators are available to get the job done and do it properly. It is more convenient for customers in terms of preparation time, therefore, it is easier to sell in both commercial and residential accounts. For residential accounts, baiting fits into seasonal and yearly pest control contracts. Less-frequent visits result in higher profits.

Baiting is perceived as more environmentally friendly than conventional pesticide applications. Baits do not adversely affect indoor air quality, nor do they belong to chemical groups with a long history of environmental groups attacking them. Plus, the Environmental Protection Agency (EPA) has recently permitted the registration of different cockroach baits to be used outdoors, indoor and in food-processing areas with few restrictions.

With these powerful forces favoring baits, is it any wonder they have made it? Interestingly enough, the few still fighting the presence of baits use the excuse that the customer will not accept them. "These customers are used to seeing a sprayer, and will quit or argue against the use of bait," they say. Whatever happened to marketing? Advanced technology? Professional perception?

For those of you using baits, this article will be of immediate use. Those of you who refuse to use cockroach baits, save this article. You will need it soon enough.

Think Like a Cockroach

Successful baiting requires "thinking like a cockroach." The tips that follow will help sharpen your baiting skills and help you select which baits to use under different circumstances.

- **Cockroaches follow edges when migrating to and from their harborage to feeding areas**—The idea is to bait along those lines and at intersections. The top of the center column in a commercial kitchen is a good example.

- **Cockroaches must have moisture to survive**—The drier an area is, the faster cockroaches come running to cockroach gels. Once the gels dry out, they lose their strong attraction, but still kill cockroaches that stumble over the dry bait.

American roach

Austin Frishman

Are You Using Sticky Traps the Right Way?

The use of sticky traps is sweeping the pest control industry, but they're not always used the right way. Some things must be learned by trial and error. A great tool in one person's hands can be a detriment in another's possession. This month's column does not address the technical aspects of sticky traps. It covers roles traps can play and some general tips on making the traps more effective.

Hot Tips

Here are twenty different ways sticky traps can be used:

1. Obtaining new work in current accounts. They can be used to help verify why extra service is needed to treat a suspended ceiling. Rather than explaining that cockroaches are present in a suspended ceiling over a dishwasher unit, show the customer with live traps or sticky boards. It reinforces with a very vivid picture why extra control is needed. It is difficult to visualize what is going on above the ceiling tiles and even more difficult to spend money for control in an area you can not see.

2. Acquiring new accounts. Installation of sticky traps in prospective accounts and following up to give "free" advice on the status of an account can land new business. Sales people can use this.

3. Assessing your own account is also important. Install the traps in your account before your competitors do.

4. Help get the customer to clean up in most necessary areas. With the sticky traps, you can pinpoint where trouble is, and visibly show the client the need to clean.

5. Aid the technician doing the account as to when to spend extra time treating. Action is needed where the cockroaches are present in sticky traps.

6. Serves as the template for your Integrated Pest Management (IPM) control. A monitoring program using sticky traps justifies why you do not have to use pesticide in the areas where there are no pests. The sticky traps verify the need or lack of need to treat.

7. Determine what products transported into an account are the culprits bringing in new cockroaches. German cockroaches stay close to the harborage area. A catch near new boxes when nothing was caught in the area in the past pinpoints suspect product. Follow up with a visual per inspection to verify this.

> Properly placing sticky traps in hidden areas conditions a technician to treat and inspect each zone where cockroaches can harbor.

8. Verifies how long each zone within an account remains pest free and if your control program is effective. Customers are hoping to learn that their home or office is in great shape, pest control wise.

9. Helps pinpoint the direction from which cockroaches are moving. By looking into the sticky trap and studying the pattern of the catch on a glue board, one can often surmise where the cockroaches are coming from.

10. Provides control without the use of any pesticides. In some situations, massive trapping, along with sealing cracks, vacuuming and improved sanitation can result in complete elimination of a cockroach population.

11. Finds other pests. When you least expect it, millipedes, mites, etc. show up, alerting you to additional arthropods in the area.

12. Advertising in a subliminal way. Each sticky trap with your company name on it can serve as a business card, reinforcing who is doing the work in an account.

13. Justify why a pesticide is used. Insects caught on a sticky trap verify the need to apply a pesticide in many cases.

14. Training tools. Collect traps from the field with items on them. Use them for an in-house identification, collection and training tool for technicians waiting to learn how to identify pests.

15. Reinforce insect phobia situations. In such suspect cases, the sticky traps serve both to determine what to treat for and why. It also shows the client you are doing something other than "spraying."

16. Quality control. A supervisor can quickly check what shape accounts are in on a per technician, per type of account basis. It saves supervisors many hours of inspections and informs pest control supervisory people what is happening before the customer knows it.

17. Determine trends in insect populations in your area. The larger the firm, the easier it is to do. Even a one-route company can find it helpful. By recording what you catch on each account and reviewing the results, it is easy to see when a pest first appears and alert other technicians and/or customers what to be on the lookout for.

18. Properly placing sticky traps in hidden areas conditions a technician to treat and inspect each zone where cockroaches can harbor.

19. Before a cleanout, sticky traps can be helpful to let you know where to concentrate your control efforts. It can also save you time and pesticide in areas where no cockroaches are present.

20. Make your baiting program more effective. It shows you where to add more bait.

Next month, we'll discuss when *not* to bait. **PC**

Austin M. Frishman, a pest control consultant since 1967, is president of AMF Pest Management Services Inc., Farmingdale, N.Y. He specializes in pest control training and inspections, research and marketing of pesticides and equipment, and insect and rodent control for a wide variety of businesses.

Austin Frishman

The American roach—high-rise headache

Approaching American cockroach control in a high-rise building requires knowledge a cut above basic training. American cockroaches, once inside a high-rise building, can easily migrate upward along pipes.

Attempting to space treat for control is one of the worst approaches that you can take. It will often result in scattering cockroaches upward and outward three stories up and further. You need to approach this methodically.

Overnight, 500 American cockroaches can enter a roach-free building. This can occur when sewers back up and the cockroaches are attempting to escape the high water table.

If boxes are stored in a basement that has cockroaches, the egg capsules can be carried upward with the boxes without detection. This can be the source of a sudden appearance of American cockroaches on four different floors, all within one week, with no apparent link among the sightings.

When trying to control American cockroaches in a high-rise building, you should first develop some basic information that will help you achieve control. Use of a compressed sprayer and a residual pest control job just do not cut it for American cockroaches.

Here are 12 basic detective questions, and the reasons for asking them, that will help you solve the infestation:

1. How long has this been going on?

If the answer is "for years," you can rely on the egg capsules having been deposited in different areas of the building, with a spread of cockroaches to upper floors. Control will now require more work and take longer before you succeed.

2. Has major construction taken place in the building?

Such action can further disperse these insects. In addition, you will want to talk to the construction personnel to inquire whether or not they saw any cockroaches.

3. Are you seeing adult cockroaches or nymphs, and if so, what size nymphs?

Adults migrate much further than the immature insects. Adults found by employees in a building can be a long way from the breeding sources.

4. Are there any rodent glue boards in the building and, if so, where are they located?

If the answer is "yes," check to see if any cockroaches have been caught on them. Over time, these boards serve well as monitoring devices. A board put down for a few days may shed some light.

5. Where is the sewer line, and are you having any problem with hook-ups?

A break in the pipe or a missing interior lid can be the source of the problem. Screen or replace the cap to stop migration into the building.

6. Are large live plants present, and if so, where?

The preferred food of American cockroaches is plant material. Plants can also be a water source. It is essential that they be checked and protected.

7. Are boxes brought up from the basement, and what's in them if they are?

Toilet paper, fluorescent bulbs, hand towels and business records are often stored in the basement. Cockroaches hide in such items and take a free ride upstairs. You must check such areas.

8. Where is the hottest, wettest area in the basement or sub-basement?

It is a likely source of the infestation.

9. Where are wet pit areas in the basement?

Again, a likely place to start looking.

10. Are you aware if any neighboring buildings are experiencing infestations?

Sometimes the sewers have heavy populations, and they are migrating into a number of nearby stores. If this is the case, capping all open pipes is essential. In addition, you may have to work on getting a large contract to treat the sewers.

11. Have any toilets been allowed to go dry because of inactivity in the area?

Dried toilet lines allow the cockroaches to move up the pipes and enter a room. By keeping water in the lines, you prevent this.

12. How many stories are there in the building, and how many sub-floors? Which locations over the past six to seven months have had sightings and how often in what area?

Plot this to help determine if any patterns exists, and determine where you need to concentrate the most to achieve control.

Once you know where and why the cockroaches are present, follow this program:

1. Treat floor drains and sewer lines with Drione dust. It may be necessary monthly.

2. Use Maxforce gel paste, AMRF 2000 boric acid paste and Avert paste in areas where cockroaches are noted. Sometimes, you do *not* want to put it in the areas where people work, but rather in wall voids, pipe chase areas and suspended ceilings. This reduces the chance of drawing insects into the open where they cause excitement.

3. Inspect all elevator pits monthly and bait as needed.

4. Examine the top of the freight elevator, and bait as needed.

5. Check the roof flanges. Flush with PT 565 plus a flushing agent. If they are found, use a residual along all such cracks.

6. To improve cockroach trap counts on sticky traps, add food product with a banana extract or food attractants.

7. Get pipe collars sealed.

8. In the South, an exterior control program is also needed as the situation dictates. **PC**

Austin M. Frishman, a pest control consultant since 1967, is president of AMF Pest Management Services Inc., Farmingdale, N.Y. He specializes in pest control training and inspections, research and marketing of pesticides and equipment, and insect and rodent control for a wide variety of businesses.

AUSTIN Frishman

How to Improve Cockroach Bait Application

As I worked in the field with technicians who are trained in baiting for cockroaches, it was interesting to see which points needed reinforcement or clarification at commercial accounts. What follows is based on actual instances where the technician was simply never taught what to do, or else forgot or overlooked them.

1 The technician was hesitant to use Maxforce bait trays. He had once encountered a local health department official who inspected more closely because the bait trays were in place. Thus, the customer did not want the trays anymore. I believe this was a communication problem. The pest management firm could solve this by inviting health department inspectors to attend its in-house training program.

2 The technicians were concerned that they would run out of cracks to keep baiting. The fact is, emphasis should be placed on refraining from unnecessary baiting, once the cockroaches are eliminated. Also, only use a *small* amount of bait in cracks.

Dr. Austin Frishman, an industry consultant since 1967, is president of AMF Pest Management Services Inc., Boca Raton, Fla. He specializes in pest management training and inspections, research and marketing of pesticides and equipment, and insect and rodent strategies for a wide variety of businesses.

3 A restaurant account repainted and remodeled. You have to re-bait after this. If new paintings are on the wall, and you baited the old paintings, you will now need to re-bait the new ones. If there are fresh flowers in the vases of the restaurant booths, you have to consider the vases to be a potential cockroach harborage area. This is especially true if each vase sits in a wicker basket.

4 Have a ladder available to bait in high places properly.

5 Sticky traps are needed to monitor what is going on—not on the initial clean-out, but on the follow-up and thereafter.

6 Hercules Putty helps bait trays to stick, but only use a small amount. Too much will result in a space behind the bait tray, which can serve as a harborage area.

7 When you bait, it is not necessary to do an ultra-low volume (ULV) treatment. If anything, it hinders the bait's effectiveness.

8 Realistically, you do not have enough time to bait every area on every service. Select a section and do it thoroughly. Move to a new area the next time. Use sticky traps to help you determine where to bait.

9 Avery Dot stickers are helpful to record the installation dates of bait trays. Change the trays once every six months. When disposing of them, be sure to place the trays in a wrapper per label directions.

10 Wear gloves. You do not want to touch surfaces where the cockroaches are running.

11 Carry a roll of paper towels to pick up spills or excess amounts of baiting gel.

12 Store all materials in one location when you enter an account. That way, you do not forget anything when you leave. A carrying case is helpful in this respect. Also, never leave your materials unattended.

13 Do not place product on a shelf storing food.

14 Bait the undersides of chairs and tables in the dining areas.

15 Don't forget to ask your customers where, when and how many cockroaches they saw at the account. Keep your log book up-to-date.

16 Cockroaches follow lines, so where columns and wires enter the suspended ceiling is an excellent place to bait.

17 Gel bait is wet. Be careful when injecting behind an electrical plate.

18 If large numbers of cockroaches are present on the initial baiting program, it is important on the next visit to re-bait this same area—the cockroaches may have eaten all of the bait.

19 Clean up dead cockroaches in ceiling light fixtures, so you can determine whether new activity is occurring. In some cases, you can clean it while inspecting.

20 Do not rely strictly on your gel bait. After the initial clean-out, the bait trays play a very important role. They can even be more effective then gel, which dries out. **PC**

PRACTICAL TIPS

QUESTIONS TO ASK BEFORE TREATING AN OFFICE BUILDING

All too often, PCOs sell their pest control services to managers of commercial office buildings over the phone. More often than not, the final sales figure is arrived at by some magical formula based on X-number of units per floor. This is a mistake. Any experienced pest control professional will tell you that to do the job properly, not to mention price the job profitably, you need to answer numerous questions *before* making the sale. Although the following list of questions is not all inclusive, they are indicative of the types of questions you should be asking building managers.

• How many floors are in the building, including basements and sub-basements? What is the major activity on each floor? (i.e. offices, storage, etc.)
• Is a simplified floor plan of the building available?
• What is the flow pattern of flourescent bulbs, toilet paper, plastic bags, towels, and soap?
• Where are coffee break areas located?
• Are office workers allowed to eat at their desks?
• Where are computer rooms located and are the computers on raised floors?
• What hours are the different areas of the building open?
• Who has the keys to specific areas of the building?
• Are there any lockers in the structure? Where are they located?
• Where are all utility areas in the building? How many are present?
• Who are the key contacts for the account and how can they be reached?
• Who is responsible for coordinating and logging in all pest sightings?
• Are there any special considerations in terms of pesticide sensitivity that the technician should be aware of?
• Do any employees in the building belong to a union? If so, what is the union's policy regarding access to lockers?
• What is the past history of pest problems in the building?
• What type of neighborhood is the structure located in?
• How many commercial food facilities are contained in the building?
• Are other pest control companies servicing a portion of the structure?
• What type of smoke detectors and alarm systems are in place?
• Where should the service technician park his/her vehicle? Is there a fee to do so?
• Will there be a language barrier when speaking to occupants of the building?
• Where is the receiving dock located?
• Where do the sewer lines enter the building?
• What are the general sanitary conditions of the building?
• Are there suspended ceilings in the building? Where and how many? How high are they? Is access fairly easy?
• If individual offices purchase bottled water, where are the bottles stored?
• How many vending machines does the building house and where are they located?
• Are employees urged to store empty soda cans for recycling?
• Does the lobby or reception area contain indoor plants, water falls, or other decorative features?
• What color are baseboards, carpeting, and other surfaces that might be treated in the future?
• Where is garbage stored and when is it removed?
• What pests are expected to be covered in the contract?
• Are any major renovations anticipated in or near the structure? If so, when?

This is only a partial list of questions the PCO should ask *before* bidding on a commercial office building account. To do anything less is not only foolhardy, but it could be terribly costly. Of course, you'll want to add some questions of your own to the list. — *Austin Frishman* ■

The author is a contributing editor to Pest Control Technology *magazine.*

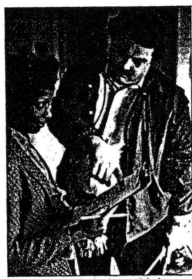

Customer communication is essential when servicing complex structures like office buildings.

For quick, easy access to manufacturers' product information, call PCT's new toll-free reader service number.

Treatment Countdown
▶ DR. AUSTIN FRISHMAN'S INDUSTRY CHECKLIST

Death, taxes and cockroach infestations

DR. AUSTIN FRISHMAN

Back in 1980, I knew how phenomenal cockroach baiting was going to be. But even then, I said, "My money is still on the cockroach."

Nothing lasts forever. Baits still work, but in a few instances — and more will occur — German cockroaches are avoiding the gel baits, regardless of whose gel it is. The different bait formulators are working hard to overcome this new challenge (case in point: the new Maxforce FC Select bait). In the meantime, I am convinced that this problem is more widespread that we are led to believe. Here are some tell-tale signs:

1. PMPs are telling each other at meetings of the large cockroach cleanouts they've done lately.
2. PMPs are reporting the roaches are not feeding on gel baits.
3. Cockroaches collected in garbage chutes and restaurants in cities like New York and Miami proved to reject cockroach gel baits.
4. Roaches are starting to appear at restaurants in plain view again. (I almost forgot what that was like.)
5. It's not just restaurants — apartment buildings are seeing bait-rejecting roach populations.

So "behavioral resistance" is happening, but it is not unexpected. My own hypothesis is that in many accounts, old bait gel is left for months. It far outnumbers the number of fresh bait locations. When roaches do enter these accounts, they test many of the old, unpalatable bait locations and "learn" to stay away from any bait gel. These educated roaches, so to speak, are able to survive and produce similar-acting roaches in the next generation.

It's pretty easy to determine whether you have a problem: Put out a few gel baits near the roaches and wait a few minutes. If they do not come to the bait and begin feeding, you have a problem.

10 STEPS TO REGAINING CONTROL

1. Do not resort to space treatments of large areas with pyrethrin. It did not work years ago, and it will not work now. It only scatters the population and increases the difficulty level to eliminate the cockroaches. It also increases the chance of triggering asthmatic attacks.
2. Rely on your sticky traps now more than ever. Use more of them, and monitor them more closely. Take even a single roach on a sticky trap seriously.
3. Look at crack and crevice products, such as those from Whitmire Micro-Gen.
4. Try to remove as much of the old bait as possible.
5. Install cockroach bait trays (such as the Roach Terminal, for example) to better protect the bait.
6. Dust voids, even using a drill to get at inaccessible voids. This may also require more than one size duster — for example, bring along a Centro bulb and an Exacticide unit.
7. Use large plastic bags to encompass and seal off harborage areas like newspaper stacks or cardboard boxes.
8. Get back to basics: Tear things apart, get on your hands and knees, climb high, get access to locked areas. Don't let the cockroaches beat you. We have come too far to slip backward.
9. Work on getting the customers' cooperation with proper sanitation and removing debris and harborage sites. They should keep garbage can lids closed, bring in outdoor pet food at night, etc.
10. Follow up within a few days after "cleanout." Install fresh sticky traps and monitor at least weekly until you are satisfied there are no more cockroaches.

Take even a single roach on a sticky trap seriously.

Regardless of what is developed to overcome bait aversion, keep in mind that the cockroaches have already developed genetic pathways to overcome baits once. They'll do it again, only next time more quickly. My money's *still* on the cockroach. **PC**

Dr. Austin Frishman, an industry consultant since 1967, is president of AMF Pest Management Services Inc., Boca Raton, FL. He specializes in pest management training and inspections, research and marketing, and insect and rodent strategies. Contact him at afrishman@advanstar.com.

Circle #136

Austin Frishman

Control From the Cockroach's Perspective

In Part I of this three-part series, we discussed the horrors of having cockroaches. In Part II, we covered the reasons the cockroaches continue to persist from different points of view. This column will cover the cockroach's perspective on the whole situation. Reasons domestic cockroaches are so successful:

1. Their ability to hide in cracks and crevices. Their body is flattened dorsal-vertically allowing them to fit readily into cracks. The early instar nymphs can pocket into the smallest cracks imaginable.

2. Their small size compared to humans allows them to hide where we cannot reach them.

3. Swiftness in adopting to changes. Think how fast a cockroach learns to survive in a microwave oven, computer, etc.

4. They can run fast.

5. They can go several days without eating or drinking.

6. They can withstand extensive temperature ranges and survive in temperatures from 30 degrees F. to 120 degrees F. For short periods of time, they can survive from 0 degrees F. and 140 degrees F.

7. Cockroaches are nocturnal and as such avoid most contact with humans.

8. They develop both behavioral and chemical resistance over a relatively short number of generations.

Austin M. Frishman, a pest control consultant since 1967, is president of AMF Pest Management Services Inc., Farmingdale, N.Y. He specializes in pest control training and inspections, research and marketing of pesticides and equipment, and insect and rodent control for a wide variety of businesses.

9. The reproductive capacity is tremendous allowing for a 90 percent death rate monthly and still increasing over time.

10. The length of the life cycle is short (at least with German cockroaches). This allows for more generations in a short time frame. Monthly service just will not cut it once a population is established.

11. The body is covered with a wax coating, helping to prevent dehydration.

12. A series of hairs project from the surface of their body that can sense the slightest noise, smell, air movement and other environmental conditions alerting the cockroach to respond quickly to any danger or adverse environmental conditions.

13. Long antennae can serve like a cane for a blind person, thereby, avoiding stepping onto detrimental surfaces.

14. They can walk upside down on surfaces without falling off.

15. They can be transported undetected in boxes, bags and pocketbooks via buses, cars, trains, planes and ships.

16. They leave a distinct spot of fecal and anal materials that serve to help locate their harborage sites. This can also help to attract new cockroaches to the area, which adds to the genetic hybrid vigor pool.

17. They can lose an appendage or two and still escape and survive.

18. They leave a chemical trail to follow for foraging.

19. Adult females, after forming an egg capsule and prior to hatching, will reduce eating and drinking, thereby, reducing the chance of getting killed, because they can remain in their harborage site.

20. Females carrying capsules congregate together and in hard-to-reach locations. For example, behind the insulation or motor of a refrigerator.

21. When harboring areas become over crowded rather than turning to cannabilism or other forms of self destruction, they migrate seeking new harborage sites.

22. Before swallowing food, they can pretaste it with mouth-part appendages. It is difficult to get a German cockroach to feed upon a toxicant-based food, but Maxforce, MRF 2000 Boric Acid Paste and Avert all have proven to be readily accepted by the German cockroach.

23. After mounting, mobility is limited. It is this time that the cockroaches are most vulnerable to outside environmental hazards.

24. The amount of moisture needed to survive is limited. This moisture can be obtained from melting snow on a boot, condensation from a window, moist soil in a potted plant, a spilled cup of coffee or moisture in toothpaste.

25. Cockroaches are omnivorous. They can survive by eating anything humans can eat as well as some plant material we cannot feed on.

26. The amount of food each cockroach feeds upon is so little that crumbs are enough for them to survive. Grease left on a can opener can support hundreds of nymphal cockroaches.

27. The German cockroach is the only domestic cockroach to carry its ootheca until ready to hatch. This limits the chance of parasitism and allows the gravid female the best environment to produce successful emergence of the offspring—a job she does well, as a 90 percent plus survival rate per egg capsule is common.

28. When hungry, they can resort to canabilism or eat their own cast skins to survive.

29. If they fall into standing water, they can swim to the edge and escape, providing the sides are not slippery and vertical.

30. Some species of cockroaches can tolerate immense population density pressures, so close that they touch each other. **PC**

Appendix II:
Cockroach Bait Aversion Q&A

Cockroach Bait Aversion Behavior

Cockroach bait aversion was an issue that was studied and overcome by research scientists at Bayer. Researchers at North Carolina State University discovered the electrophysiological conformation of the alterations in the contact chemoreceptors in cockroach palpi. Certainly cockroaches will continue to challenge man's control efforts and we will need to continue to work to stay ahead of roaches. Below Dr. Byron Reid, Head of Bayer Environmental Sciences Product Development Department, shares his insights on this subject.

PHOTO 15.1: **Cockroaches have two pair of external taste receptor palpi. A successful bait must successfully get past these palpi prior to entering the roach's mouth where additional sensory organs exist. Photo by Anthony Bello.**

Q: Is cockroach bait aversion a phenomenon your researchers were already aware of?
A: The original case of bait aversion from the late 1980's was - in fact - discovered by Maxforce researchers in the United States. Prof. Jules Silverman, one of the authors in this current paper on mutations in taste receptors of German cockroaches, worked for Maxforce in the 80s and 90s and was the lead investigator in the pioneering research performed by Maxforce on bait aversion before joining the faculty at North Carolina State University. So it should come as no surprise when we say that Bayer is very much aware of the problems with bait aversion in German cockroaches. We have been working both to understand and solve the problem of bait aversion in the German cockroach for more than 25 years!

Q: Is this aversion problem limited to cockroaches only in the United States or is there similar evidence of this behavior elsewhere in the world?
A: To date, bait aversion is limited to only one species of cockroach, the German cockroach, but this species has spread world-wide and is a top pest in most countries. There is

absolutely no biological reason to expect that bait aversion is limited only to the US, and Bayer suspects that this phenomenon is present in many parts of the world to one degree or another. Discussion of bait aversion has certainly gathered more attention in the US, but is this because control strategies in the US differ so radically from elsewhere in the world, or is this because most of the world's top experts on German cockroaches are located in the US?

Q: Do your cockroach bait products include glucose or other attractants that may cause aversion? And, if so, is this latest report cause for concern?

A: No, this latest report does not cause any concern to Bayer and here is why. It important for your readers to understand that the recent publicity was not a link to the discovery of bait aversion, since we've known about bait aversion for more than 25 years! This latest report was significant, however, because now researchers at North Carolina State University had finally identified the mechanism by which German cockroaches detected and avoided glucose in in gel baits. You see, the specific strain of German cockroaches used in the research (known as the T-164 strain) was the very same strain collected in Florida by Dr. Silverman and his Maxforce research colleagues in the late 1980s. In response to that original discovery, Maxforce cockroach gels were reformulated in the mid-1990s to overcome glucose avoidance behavior in German cockroaches. However, by the year 2000 Bayer started getting reports from the field that sounded like another round of bait aversion was happening, and sure enough we found several strains of German cockroaches that were no longer responding to fructose (a replacement sugar in most cockroach gel baits); some of these strains had also developed aversion to a few non-food ingredients in the formulation. It was in response to this second outbreak of bait aversion that Bayer developed our now familiar formulation in Maxforce FC Select and Maxforce FC Magnum and sold in other brands all over the world. This bait matrix is the culmination of 20 years of research on cockroach gel baits and of course we at Bayer believe it is the very best formulation on the market today.

Q: What plans do you have to amend your formulations?

A: As we've hopefully conveyed in our earlier answers, Bayer is always working to improve our bait formulations. The cockroaches are not likely going to cooperate; we will always have work to keep ahead of them. Those who are worried about bait aversion, or who may have a difficult to control infestation and suspect bait aversion, can count of the Maxforce cockroach gels to give them the best chance to gain control, not only of the everyday cockroaches but of those difficult to control populations as well. At Bayer, we know the German cockroach will continue to respond to our efforts to control them, so we must remain vigilant for the emergence of more complicated cases of bait aversion, and also guard against classic resistance to the insecticides we use in our bait formulations.

Best regards,

Dr. Byron Reid, Ph.D.
Bayer ES Development

Q: Was bait aversion an issue for your company's bait products? What research and development work was conducted by Syngenta to address cockroach bait aversion behavior?

A: Bait aversion is an issue for the industry, and it is a leading reason why Advion® cockroach gel bait was developed in 2006. The formulation was heavily researched and evaluated over several years. It was determined that a combination of ingredients makes the bait very attractive to all cockroach species, including strains of German cockroaches that had developed behavioral resistance to existing commercial gel products. Much of the research and development work invested in the Advion formulation focused on very specific ingredients and/or combinations of ingredients that would trigger averse behavior in cockroaches. This work required using dozens of field-collected strains that exhibited averse behavior.

Q: Is cockroach resistance to pesticides an ongoing issue? How are Syngenta scientists working to address resistance issues of the future?

A: As part of our stewardship for new technologies, Syngenta Professional Pest Management trains Pest Management Professionals (PMPs) on best practices to avoid the development of resistance. To maintain product leadership in the marketplace and stay ahead of any potential performance issues, Syngenta has invested in one of the largest and most intense German cockroach resistance management programs in the industry. By partnering with Dr. Mike Scharf and Purdue University over the last seven years, we have developed a robust resistance monitoring program that has been highlighted in two recent scientific publications [(Ameya D Gondhalekar, Cheol Song and Michael E Scharf, 2011. Pest Man. Sci. 67:262-270), and (AMEYA D. GONDHALEKAR, CLAY W. SCHERER, RAJ K. SARAN, AND MICHAEL E. SCHARF, 2013. JEE, 106:945-953.)]. We invested in these research efforts to provide PMPs with topnotch technical support and to ensure our products meet performance expectations.

Q: Are there any new silver bullet type products that will be introduced for cockroach control in the next few years? What do you see as the future of cockroach control?

A: The management of German cockroaches is very challenging and requires a true Integrated Pest Management (IPM) approach. This includes proper inspection/monitoring, sanitation, proper use of control measures, communication with clients and continued education. Our products perform very well, but are only a part of a total management solution.

The responses above were provided by **Dr. Clay W. Sherer** of the Syngenta Product Development Team.

©2013 Syngenta. **Important: Always read and follow label instructions. Some products may not be registered for sale or use in all states or counties. Please check with your state or local Extension Service to ensure registration status.** Advion® and the Syngenta logo are trademarks of a Syngenta Group Company. Syngenta Customer Center: 1-866-SYNGENT(A) (796-4368).

The Advance(R) and Alpine(R) cockroach baits were developed for and tested on the common strains of bait averse cockroaches as well as susceptible strains. And, while these products represent the state of the art, the long term solution to gel aversion lies in an integrated approach to baiting. The industry needs to move away from its heavy reliance on gel as its single silver bullet. BASF offers two different gel matrices each containing different food components for rotation, and offers a dry flowable bait formulation that removes some of the dependency on gel in bait focused programs. Additional bait formulations continue to be developed and researched using novel attractants.

The use of non-repellent residual insecticides is emerging as a successful adjunct to baits. Phantom and Alpine products have been shown to not disrupt normal feeding on gel baits, even when applied directly over the bait placement. This creates new possibilities for a more fully integrated approach to cockroach control when considering resistance management, especially when faced with the harsh environments in commercial kitchens that materials need to be able to withstand.

The biggest challenges with cockroach management continues to be the intensive attention to detail when inspecting and applying a treatment to all those difficult to reach harborages. Advanced monitoring techniques to assist with inspections is the future of cockroach control, as well as new methods of making targeted treatments easier to apply.

Brian Mann
Marketing Manager
Pest Control Solutions
BASF The Chemical Company

Appendix III: Sponsors

Environmental Delivery Sytems, Inc.
Contact: Eddie Evans
P.O. Box 1777
Friendswood, TX 77549
1-877-ACTISOL (228-4765)

Website: www.actisol.com

Manufacturer of the Actisol® Brand of Mechanical Aerosol Generators and Spray Equipment.

Serving the pest management industry for more than 25 years, Environmental Delivery Systems, Inc. is a world leader in the design and production of mechanical aerosol generators and custom application equipment. In addition, we repair and recondition application equipment, including foggers, compressed air sprayers, dusters, and foamers.

The products and services we offer continue to provide pest management professionals with unmatched quality and dependability essential to their success. With a worldwide distribution network, we provide our customers with easy access to our products and services.

WHAT IS ACTISOL®?

A high quality, low maintenance mechanical device that combines the capacity of refillable hand sprayers, the treatment capability of misters and foggers, with the convenience and simplicity of prepackaged aerosols. These systems are designed to create optimum sized uniform insecticide particles and force them into difficult to reach harborage areas such as, ceiling and wall voids, food preparation areas and equipment, as well as cracks and crevices where insect pests live and multiply.

ABOUT ACTISOL®?

No matter how you slice it, the Actisol® insecticide delivery systems simply outperform most other application methods by utilizing an advanced design that has a number of distinct advantages. These advantages include the safe and effective elimination of insects while using non-residual insecticides and forcing ideally-sized insecticide particles to reach insects in deep harborage with a constant flow of low pressure, high volume, clean compressed air.

Actisol® Compact Unit

B290300

Length	13.5"
Width	6.75"
Height	7.00"
Weight (empty)	16 lbs.
Weight (full)	17.5 lbs.
Shipping Weight	21lbs.
Tank Capacity	28 oz
Discharge Hose Length	15 ft.
Spray Output	0.49 oz/minute @ 12psi
Operating Pressure (liquid)	12 - 20 psi
Operating Pressure (air)	20 psi
Droplet Size (average)	10 micron
Droplet Size (range)	2.4 – 20+ micron
Motor	110 V AC, 50 Hz, 3amps
Compressor Type	diaphragm

- Deliver Aerosol & Residual Products
- Residential & Small Commercial Accounts
- Bedbugs, Cockroaches, Bees, Ants, Stored Product, Pests, Termites
- Perfect for Sensitive Situations
- *Available with anodized tank and chassis for protection when using water based formulations.*

Actisol® Commercial Unit

B290400

Length	18"
Width	21"
Height	34"
Weight (empty)	48 lbs.
Weight (full)	57 lbs.
Shipping Weight	70 lbs.
Tank Capacity	80 oz.
Discharge Hose Length	50 ft.
Spray Output	0.56 oz./minute @ 15psi
Operating Pressure (liquid)	15 - 30 psi
Operating Pressure (air)	35 psi
Droplet Size (average)	10 micron
Droplet Size (range)	2.4 – 30+ micron
Motor	110 V AC, 50 Hz, 2.9amps
Compressor Type	oil-less Rocking Piston

- Deliver Aerosol & Residual Products
- Commercial Accounts
- Food Processing Facilities
- Hospitals
- Warehouses
- Amusement Parks
- Hotels
- Perfect for Sensitive Situations

Actisol® Perimeter Pro

B390100

Depth	19"
Width	21"
Height	37"
Height (Handle Extended)	48"
Weight (empty)	52 lbs.
Shipping Weight	63 lbs.
Tank Capacity	7 gal.
Fill Hose Length (Blue)	20 ft.
Discharge Hose Length (Red)	20 ft.
Spray Output	1.5 gpm
Spray Pattern	Full Cone to Pin Stream
Pump	ShurFlo 8000 Series
Pump Type	12 VDC, 3.6 — 6.8amps
Battery	12V/12A.H.
	Rechargeable Sealed Lead Acid

- Exterior Perimeter Applications
- Termiticide Applications
- Green House Applications
- Weed Control
- Liquid Fertilizer Applications
- Amusement Parks & Sports Arenas
- Hotels
- Perfect for Sensitive Situations

ENVIRONMENTAL DELIVERY SYSTEMS, INC.   WWW.ACTISOL.COM   1-877-ACTISOL (228-4765)

ABOUT AMVAC

AMVAC Chemical Corporation is a leading developer and manufacturer of agricultural and commercial products for crop protection applications as well as commercial and public health uses.

With four manufacturing facilities in the US as well as 90 patents on products in 60 countries, AMVAC delivers quality products with an excellent regulatory record and a focus on environmental protection and environmental stewardship. AMVAC's mission is clear—to help farmers improve crop growth and yield to better meet the world's food needs as well as increase quality of life for global citizens through agricultural support and public health products.

AMVAC PRODUCTS

Nuvan® Prostrips®

Nuvan® Prostrips® are long lasting, odorless strips that effectively rid tough to reach areas of cockroaches. Each Nuvan® Prostrip® may be selectively placed or hung, protecting enclosed areas for up to four months with a single application. They are the only product containing DDVP labeled for residential use.

Wisdom® Line

Wisdom® products are pyrethroid insecticides that contain bifenthrin to control and combat cockroaches. They can be used both indoors and outdoors.

- Wisdom® EZ
- Wisdom® Flowable
- Wisdom® Lawn Granular
- Wisdom® Nursery Granular
- Wisdom® TC Flowable

PRELUDE® Termiticide/Insecticide

PRELUDE® Termiticide/Insecticide is a general use, indoor and outdoor spray with permethrin to effectively control cockroaches.

ORTHENE® PCO Pellets

ORTHENE® PCO Pellets mix easily with water to create a powerful spray for use within industrial, institutional and commercial buildings, including restaurants, warehouses, stores, hospitals, hotels, manufacturing plants and ships to effectively combat cockroaches.

AMVAC

For more information about AMVAC products, call **1-888 GO AMVAC (1-888-462-6822)** or visit **www.amvac-chemical.com**.

Field Sales Team: Rennie Kubik, Dean May, John Boltin, John Bruce, Ron Johnson, Peter Connelly, Jeff Alvis and Ted Smith

Product Development: Chuck Silcox

Always read and follow all label directions and use precautions. Turfcide® is a registered trademark of AMVAC Chemical Corporation. ©2013 AMVAC Chemical Corporation.

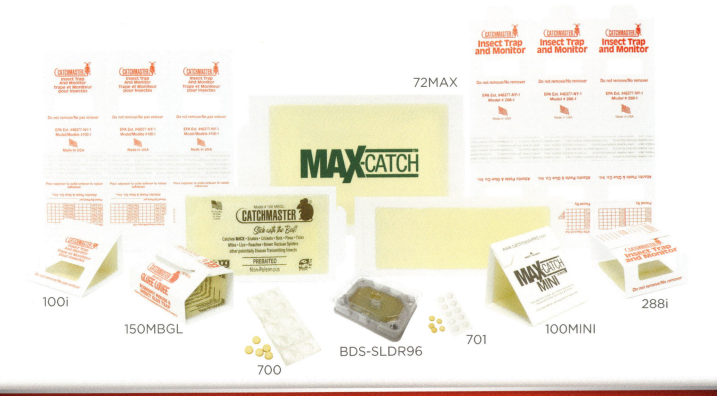

Catchmaster® offers a variety of insect traps and monitors, some of which are pre-baited with food grade attractants. Catchmaster® roach attractant tablets are an effective addition to any glue board or insect monitor. AP&G's knowledge of adhesive technology ensures that the Catchmaster® brand represents the gold standard of quality and consistency.

Through the continuing growth and development of the Catchmaster® line, AP&G is committed to supplying the Pest Management Industry with innovative, dependable, high value pest management products.

Visit Us Online For More Information

www.catchmasterPRO.com
info@catchmasterPRO.com
1-800-458-7454

 ATRIX INTERNATIONAL INCORPORATED

The Atrix Omega GREEN Supreme
IMMEDIATE CONTAINMENT HEPA FILTER CARTRIDGE!

Why just kill bugs with messy chemicals and heat when you can quickly and safely eliminate them with an Atrix Omega Green Supreme Vacuum?

QUIET! Less than 70 dB!

Optional Backpack Harness

Attachments Store Conveniently in Lid

Increase your service, increase your revenue!

The Omega GREEN Supreme IPM vacuum is the true *professional's* IPM tool. The immediate containment "True" HEPA filter and powerful motor safely and effectively eliminate both alive and dead pests along with their eggs and feces. The vacuum fits perfectly in the cab of a truck, and can be used on nearly every job a Professional Pest Manager goes on.

→ Filtration - Features an immediate containment True HEPA Filter Cartridge that virtually eliminates the risk of exhausting dangerous bacteria, the potentially fatal hantavirus, out into the air you and your customers breathe. Most odors are contained. Hose and filter plugs also come standard.

→ Powerful and Quiet - Will capture everything from bed bugs to cockroaches and even hazardous particles, with built in sound suppressing technology.

Made in the USA, 3 Year Limited Warranty

Part Numbers:

VACOMEGASIPM (clear hose)
VACOMEGASIPMB (black hose)

HEPA Filter: OF612HE
HEPA Filter, 4 Pack: OF612HE-4

Certifications:

The Ultra Fine Vacuum Cleaner Company...Since 1981

www.atrix.com   952-894-6154   800-222-6154   sales@atrix.com
1350 Larc Industrial Blvd, Burnsville MN 55337

Combat cockroaches with help from BASF!

Controlling cockroaches can be a challenge. They are pervasive, elusive and prolific. They reproduce quickly and prefer to live inside difficult-to-access cracks, crevices and voids. Additionally, some cockroach strains are resistant to common insecticides, and others have developed feeding aversions to bait formulations. And these challenges can be compounded by overreliance on a single product or application method.

Every cockroach solution from BASF Pest Control Solutions is designed with unique attributes that makes it effective.

BASF
The Chemical Company

Prescription Treatment® brand Avert® Dry Flowable Cockroach Bait Formula 1

Bait deep cracks or voids exceptionally well with Prescription Treatment® brand **Avert**® Dry Flowable Cockroach Bait Formula 1. Its unique dry food matrix flows deep into these harborages, where it remains attractive and active for extended periods. Cockroaches are exposed to its active ingredient, abamectin, when they eat the attractive matrix or groom themselves after tracking through **Avert Dry Flowable** deposits.

Prescription Treatment® brand Alpine® Dust Insecticide

Prescription Treatment® brand **Alpine**® **Dust Insecticide** is the industry's first and only Reduced Risk* nonrepellent dust for long-lasting, broad-spectrum control of cockroaches and other insects. It has a flexible label for inside and outside non-food handling areas, and is lightweight for better coverage and more applications per pound than other dusts.

*All **Alpine** formulations contain the active ingredient dinotefuran, a nonrepellent active that the U.S. Environmental Protection Agency has granted reduced-risk status for public health use.

Phantom® termiticide-insecticide

The only liquid nonrepellent, non-IGR labeled for indoor general pest control including the toughest conditions within commercial food handling facilities. Thanks to its cutting-edge chemistry and active ingredient chlorfenapyr, **Phantom**® **termiticide-insecticide** is proven effective on pyrethroid-resistant cockroaches, and is undetectable to these insects. As a result, cockroaches unknowingly contact and ingest it as they go about their routine activities. Additionally, **Phantom termiticide-insecticide**, with its nonrepellent formulation, won't interfere with bait placements on or around the treated spot.

Prescription Treatment® brand Alpine® Cockroach Gel Bait

Prescription Treatment® brand **Alpine**® **Cockroach Gel Bait** uses a unique matrix proven attractive to German cockroaches—even strains associated with feeding aversion to some other gels. This easy-application product starts killing roaches within hours, and is approved for use in food handling areas. Prescription Treatment brand **Alpine Cockroach Gel Bait** is available in reservoir or piston can forms.

Prescription Treatment® brand Phantom® Pressurized Insecticide

Prescription Treatment® brand **Phantom**® **Pressurized Insecticide** is known for its long-lasting effectiveness, even on harsh surfaces. This ready-to-use formulation reduces pesticide load, overuse and eliminates mixing and cleanup; formulation dries in "crystals" for enhanced bioavailability, and leaves no visible residue. It kills cockroaches on contact in commercial accounts and is approved for use in food handling and non-food-handling areas for commercial accounts. And, its nonrepellent formula will not scatter roaches during a treatment and/or disrupt cockroach feeding behavior should bait placements be nearby.

Read the **SmartSolutions for German Cockroaches Guide** on **pestcontrol.basf.us** to develop a cockroach combat approach for maximum control of the toughest cockroaches. Or visit **pestcontrol.basf.us** for more information.

Contact Information:
Bob Davis, Market Development Specialist, BASF Pest Control Solutions
e: robert.davis@basf.com   p: (512) 989-5618

Users must always read and follow label directions.
© 2013 BASF Corporation. All rights reserved.

MAXFORCE® ROACH CONTROL SYSTEM

A ROACH CONTROL SYSTEM MORE ADAPTABLE THAN ROACHES THEMSELVES.

Learn more at MaxforceRoachSystem.com

Bayer CropScience LP, Environmental Science Division, 2 TW Alexander Drive, Research Triangle Park, NC 27709. 1-800-331-2867. www.BackedbyBayer.com. Bayer (reg'd), the Bayer Cross (reg'd),

CLEAN OUT

Maxforce® FC Magnum
- Kills in hours
- Magnified Domino Effect® with a quaternary kill
- Five times more fipronil

MAINTENANCE

Maxforce FC Select
- Kills in 48 hours
- Active through contact + ingestion
- Domino Effect with a tertiary kill

Maxforce FC roach stations
- Kills in under 72 hours
- Lasts up to one year or until bait is completely consumed

ROTATION

Maxforce roach bait (with hydramethylnon)
- Delayed mortality kill
- Active through ingestion
- Domino Effect with a secondary kill
- Contaminated feces from one exposed roach will kill up to 44 others

Maxforce roach stations
- Kills in under 72 hours
- Lasts up to one year or until bait is completely consumed

and Maxforce (reg'd) are registered trademarks of Bayer. Not all products are registered in all states. Always read and follow label instructions carefully. ©2013 Bayer CropScience LP.

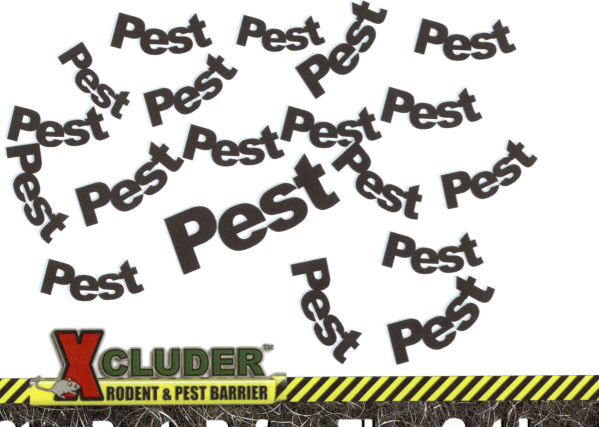

KILLS COCKROACHES.
Combat Manual Approved!

No. 217P
17.5 oz. Aerosol
6 Per Case

FAMILY OWNED AND OPERATED

JT EATON™
SINCE 1932

1-800-321-3421
www.jteaton.com

GOOD THINGS COME TO THOSE WHO BAIT
WITH THE #1 US GRANULAR BAIT

NIBAN®

Niban offers pest management professionals a perimeter bait that stands alone and practically eradicates call backs. Its active ingredient is a 5% boric acid. Each granule carries a patented formula of food attractants and food grade oils to give the bait not only excellent cockroach attraction and efficacy, but also long-term protection from mold or moisture spoilage.

Niban has long been known as a cockroach solution. It kills and controls cockroach populations from large-scale uses such as a giant New England "stump dump" for American cockroaches to the interiors of homes for German cockroaches. As a defense, cockroaches can develop resistance to pesticides in just a few generations. But because Niban works by interrupting the insect's digestive process and leaves major systems unaffected, pests can't build a tolerance, so there is no known resistance.

- Listed pests include cockroaches (Asian, American, Brown, Brown Banded, Smokey Brown, German and Oriental), multiple species of ants and crickets, silverfish, earwigs, slugs and snails.
- Weatherized: Will not degrade in heat or sunlight and lasts through 4" of rain without molding.
- Part of your Green Pest Management® program.

Visit www.nisuscorp.com to see all cockroach products offered by Nisus, including:

Labels are printed in black & white to be discrete in the field.

OMRI™ Listed
Organic Materials Review Institute

May be used as an insecticide for structural pest control provided there is no direct contact with food or crops being certified.

Nisus® CORPORATION
Green Pest Control Solutions

800.264.0870 • www.nisuscorp.com

Niban, Niban-FG, Nibor-D, Fireback, Green Pest Management and Nisus Corporation are registered trademarks of Nisus Corporation. ©2013 Nisus Corporation #CCM-NI-0813

Oldham chemicals company, inc

Consistently Meeting the Needs and Surpassing Expectations

- Complete Inventory of Chemicals with same day shipping

- Custom Spray Rigs

- Knowledgeable Staff

- 14 Regional Service Centers

www.OldhamChem.com

1-800-888-5502

PestManagement
PROFESSIONAL
PMP: The industry's leading technical journal since 1933

Congrats, Doc & Paul!

Finally …
A sequel that improves on the initial work of art!

INTEGRATED PEST MANAGEMENT STARTS HERE

AN ENVIRONMENTALLY-SAFE WAY TO EFFECTIVELY ELIMINATE PESTS

SUPER COACH PRO™
- Improved comfort and range of motion
- Increased filtration levels

GOFREE™ PRO
- Cordless efficiency
- Enhanced mobility

LINEVACER®
- Certified HEPA
- Capture and containment of pests and fecal matter

Pest Buster.
Why do ProTeam backpack vacuums work better against pests? Count the ways.

1. **Environmentally safe.** Using no chemicals or toxins, ProTeam vacuums permanently remove pests from a space.

2. **Routine elimination.** ProTeam backpack vacuums allow cleaning workers to move through a space up to 3 times faster and 44 percent more effectively, so pest management becomes routine.

3. **Immediate impact.** Instantly capture pests and contain the allergens, eggs and waste they leave behind.

4. **Versatile control.** ProTeam's IPM toolkit and high-performance design can control a wide range of pests, including bed bugs, spiders, cockroaches, wasps, beetles, box elder bugs and more.

PROPER PEST CONTROL
will help prevent or remove pests that can trigger asthma.

Source: www.pestworld.org

In any integrated pest management (IPM) system, a high-performance ProTeam vacuum is a vital tool. ProTeam vacuums combine high-powered suction with HEPA and exclusive Four Level® Filtration to capture and contain up to 99.97 percent of particulates down to 0.3 microns in size – including dead and live specimens, and allergens like cast skins and fecal matter.

In the fight against pests, ProTeam vacuums simply work better.

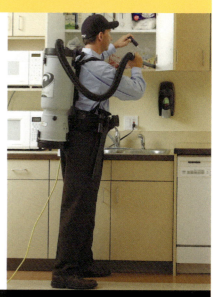

customerservice.proteam@emerson.com // proteam.com // 866.888.2168

UNFAIR ADVANTAGE
OVER COCKROACHES

At Rockwell Labs, we are obsessed with creating and manufacturing the highest quality products to give you the Unfair Advantage in the field. It begins with our baits, by using food ingredients that are different from other roach baits in order to prevent bait aversion. We also understand bait palatability is crucial for acceptance, which is why we don't mass produce our bait and allow it to sit in warehouses for extended periods of time. Rockwell baits are made just in time and shipped fresh to our distributors. We also carefully chose the powerful active ingredients, imidacloprid and abamectin, so you get the best results in the least amount of time.

Dust insecticides are an essential tool for long term cockroach control. We are not satisfied with simply offering a dust like other companies. At Rockwell, we take the extra step of milling BorActin™ to an extremely fine powder using pharmaceutical grade milling equipment to give you the best results possible. We also developed CimeXa™, the most powerful, flexible, and longest lasting desiccant insecticide available. CimeXa is non-repellent, super light, and kills much faster than diatomaceous earth. Unlike other dust insecticides, CimeXa can even be mixed with water and applied as a wettable powder and has a 10 year residual, when left undisturbed.

Rockwell products are born from science and a dedication to the pest management professional so you will have the best tools available and an Unfair Advantage.

American Owned
American Made

816-283-3167 • **www.rockwelllabs.com**

InVict, Xpress, CimeXa, BorActin, Unfair Advantage and Creating the Future of Pest Control are trademarks of Rockwell Labs Ltd. ©2013 Rockwell Labs Ltd

Proud sponsor of The Cockroach Combat Manual II.

PROFESSIONAL PEST MANAGEMENT

YOU'LL LIKE HOW FLEXIBLE IT IS. PESTS WON'T.

Arilon® Insecticide is one of the most flexible non-pyrethroid products available. You can apply it indoors and out as a spot or crack-and-crevice treatment. Plus you can make perimeter applications with it, all the way up to a 10-foot band. But no matter where you apply it, Arilon will provide comprehensive protection. That's because exposed pests can carry it back and share it with more pests. So your applications go even further, and your customers' lives go on uninterrupted.

FOR LIFE UNINTERRUPTED™

Learn more at SyngentaPMP.com/Arilon

Arilon® Insecticide

©2013 Syngenta. **Important:** Always read and follow label instructions before buying or using Syngenta products. All products may not be registered for sale or use in all states. Please check with your state or local Extension Service before buying or using Syngenta products. Arilon®, For Life Uninterrupted™, the Alliance Frame, the Purpose Icon and the Syngenta logo are trademarks of Syngenta Group Company. Syngenta Customer Center: 1-866-SYNGENT(A) (796-4368). MW 1LGP3017-P1-R1 6/13

PROFESSIONAL PEST MANAGEMENT

NOBODY SEES WHICH GEL YOU USE. JUST IF IT WORKS.

Advion® Cockroach gel bait is proven to be the most effective product of its kind. The bait matrix stays highly palatable to cockroaches for as long as three months, even to gel-averse species. And the active ingredient can only be triggered in target species after a slight delay, which gives an exposed cockroach time to share it with up to 54 other cockroaches via secondary and tertiary contact. So they multiply your control. And you get life back to normal.

FOR LIFE UNINTERRUPTED™

Learn more at SyngentaPMP.com/Advion Cockroach

© 2013 Syngenta. Important: Always read and follow label instructions. Some products may not be registered for sale or use in all states or counties. Please check with your state or local extension service to ensure registration status. Advion,® For Life Uninterrupted,™ the Alliance frame, the Purpose icon and the Syngenta logo are trademarks of a Syngenta Group Company. Syngenta Customer Center: 1-866-SYNGENT(A) (796-4368).   MW 1LGP3045-P1

Victor® Roach Pheromone Trap
A New Technology in Roach Control!

M330 Roach Pheromone Trap

- **Patented** German cockroach pheromone attractant lures them from their harborage.
- **Three entry points** provides roaches multiple access to trap.
- **Silicone surface** prevents escape.
- **Low profile** for placement in small, tight corners.
- **Excellent for IPM** program. Most accurate early warning and detection device available - not just a monitor.
- **Traps** adults, nymphs and eggs.
- **Backed** by 5 years of research and field testing.

For more information visit
www.woodstreampro.com
or call (800) 800-1819

To order contact your authorized Woodstream Pro Distributor.

Ordering Information:
M330   Roach Pheromone Trap
        48 Victor® Roach Trap Units
        (96 placements)

Woodstream Corp. 69 N. Locust St. Lititz, PA 17543

Appendix IV:
Acknowledgments, References, and Resources

Bennett, Gary W., Robert M. Corrigan, and John M. Owens. "Truman's Scientific Guide to Pest Management Operations." 4th, 5th, 6th, and 7th editions. Questex Media

Cornwell, P.B.. "The Cockroach Volume 1." Hutchinson and Company.

Frishman, Austin M. and Arthur P. Schwartz. "The Cockroach Combat Manual." William Morrow and Company.

Mallis, Arnold. *Handbook of Pest Control.* 5th, 6th, 7th, 8th, and 9th editions. GIE Media.

Smith, Eric H. and Richard C. Whitman. *NPCA Field Guide to Structural Pests.* National Pest Management Association, Inc.

Snetsinger, Robert. *The Ratcatcher's Child.* Franzak & Foster Company.

Useful Websites

The following websites may be relied upon to provide accurate and useful information. Depending upon which website you visit, you may need to navigate, click around, or enter search information to find the bed bug related information you seek.

Australian Environmental Pest Managers Association
www.aepma.com.au

Bed bug General
www.bed buggeneral.com

Center for Disease Control (CDC)
www.cdc.gov

University of Florida Department of Entomology and Nemotology
www.entnemdept.ufl.edu

Mayo Clinic
www.mayoclinic.com

National Pest Management Association
www.pestworld.org/aepma

University of Kentucky Department of Entomology
www.ca.uky.edu

Ohio State University Department of Entomology
www.entomology.osu.edu

Virginia Tech University Department of Entomology
www.ento.vt.edu

University of Minnesota Department of Entomology
www.entomology.umn.edu

Pest Management Professional Magazine
www.mypmp.com

Pest Control Technology Magazine
www.pctonline.com

The following industry colleagues have provided assistance, support and may be relied upon for their knowledge, experience and professionalism:

Barile, Joe, BCE Technical Service Lead, PPM/Vector North America Bayer Environmental Science Mansfield, MA joe.barile@bayer.com www.backedbybayer.com
Baker, Dale, VP JT Eaton, db@eaton.com
Boltin, John, Sr. Sales Representative, AMVAC, Tampa, FL 813-620-7606
Borden, Richard, Jr. Operations manager, Borden Pest Control, Inc. North Augusta, SC www.bordenpestcontrol.com Richard@bordenpestcontrol.com
Braness, Dr. Gary, Ph.D. Braness Consulting. Fresno, CA
Bruesch, Jay, BCE, Technical Director, Plunkett's Pest Control, Inc. 40 NE 52nd Way, Fridley, MN 55421 763-571-7100 www.plunketts.net jay@plnketts.net
Butler, Brian, CFO/COO, Skyline Pest Solutions, Inc., www.skylinepest.com, brian.butler@skylinepest.com
Campbell, Thomas F. Trial Lawyer, Campbell Law PC, A Purpose Filled Practice, Birmingham, Al., www.campbelllitigation.com
Church, Charlie President, Getem Services Termite & Pest Control, Virginia Beach, VA
Cicchetti, Janice A. BCE Lake Grove, NY
Clark, Garey President, Clark Pest Remedy, McDonough, GA www.clarkpestremedy.com gclark@clarkpestremedy.com
Coffelt, Dr. Mark, Development Manager, Syngenta, marl.coffelt@syngenta.com
Comis, Pete, Sales Manager, Bayer Crop Science, Research Triangle Park, NC www.bayer.com 919-549-2508
Connally, Kevin J. Sales Manager Mid-Atlantic, 2932 Catlett Rd. Charlottesville, VA 22901 434-245-0042 kevin.connally@bayer.com
Daniels, Ray, Product Manager, Bayer, ray.daniels@bayer.com
Davis, Dr. Robert, Development Manager, BASF, Robert.davis@basf.com
Dean, Jeff, Sales Manager, MGK, Dallas, TX www.mgk.com 210-213-6743
Delaney, Jim, Central Region Manager, Univar, James.Delaney@univarusa.com
Depuy, Steven Service Manager Fischer Environmental Mandeville, LA www.fischerenv.com
Deutsch, Mike, BCE, Arrow Exterminators, Lynbrook, NY, 516-593-7770
Diggs, Richard President, Alexandria Pest Services, Inc. Alexandria, VA 22306 www.alexandriapestservices.com Rdiggs@alexandriapestservices.co

Diggs, Ricky VP, Alexandria Pest Services, Inc. Alexandria, VA 703-923-0925

Douglen, Leonard Executive Director NJPMA & NYPMA, PO Box 24, Livingston, NJ 973-994-2331, nipcassoc@aol.com

Fieler, Dr. William, Formulation Chemist, American Vanguard Chemical Company, Newport Beach, CA

Fries, Susan, President, Ecola Termite & Pest Management Services, Southern & Central, CA www.ecolatermite.com 800-332-2847

Frank, Lynn, Technical Director, Suburban Exterminating, Smithtown, NY, lfrank@suburbanexterminating.com

Frisch, Jonathan, President, Atlantic Paste & Glue/Catchmaster, Brooklyn, NY www.catchmasterpro.com 718-492-3648

Frost, Dorothy A. Vice President, Abalon Exterminating Co., Inc., NYC, Dfrost@abolonexterminating.com

Gangloff-Kaufman, Dr. Jody, Ph.D. NYS IPM Program, Babylon, NY 631-539-8680

Goldstein, Michael Sales Manager Professional Products Woodstream 69 N. Locust St. Lititz, PA 17543 mgoldstein@woodstream.com

Gooch, Heather VP, Gooch & Gooch, LLC www.goochandgooch.com heather@goochandgooch.com

Grippi, Joe, Area Sales Manager, Bayer Environmental Science, Austin, TX 512-569-1069 www.backedbtbayer.com , joe.grippi@bayer.com

Hafley, Martyn, BCE Sales Director, Winfield Solutions, 1431 Greenway Drive, Suite 450, Irving, TX 75038 469-916-4030 office 817-313-4416 cell mnhafley@LandOLakes.com

Halbrook, Paul, Web Designer, paul@paulhalbrook.com

Hancock, Andrea, VP Mattress Safe and Bed Bug General, www.mattresssafe.com, www.bedbuggeneral.com, 770-205-5335

Honess, Sandra, VP Ladybug Pest Management, Delmar,DE 302-846-2295

Jamison, Don S. President/Owner Jamison Lawn & Pest Control. 3638 Summer Ave. Memphis, TN 38122 jamisonllc@aol.com

Jones, Ellis Equipment manager; Oldham Chemicals Co., Inc.; www.oldhamequip.com; ellisjones@oldhamchem.com; 800 888-5502

Knox, Justin, VP Knox Pest Control, Columbus, GA www.knoxpest.com 706-628-5599

Koehler, Dr. Phillip, Ph.D. University of Florida Department of Entomology, Gainesville, FL

Kells, Dr. Stephen A. Associate Professor, University of Minnesota, Department of Entomology, St. Paul, MN kells002@umn.edu, www.bedbugs.umn.edu

Kmetz, Steve, President, Certified Pest Control, Clevelend, OH, www.certifiedpestcontrol.com

Kubik, Rennie Senior Sales Representative, Amvac Environmental Products 360-546-5954 office 360-921-8019 cell Renniek@amvac.net

Kunst, Robert L. President, Fischer Environmental Services www.fischerenv.com robertlkunst@fischerenv.com 985-626-7378

Lee, Kathryn A. "Kitty" Sales & Service Manager Residex, LLC 134 Charlotte Ave. Hicksville, NY 11801 www.residex.com hicksville@residex.com

Lentz, Eric Head of Marketing - Pest Management, Bayer Environmental Science, eric.lentz@bayer.com

Maestre, Ralph H. BCE Technical Director, Magic Pest Management LLC, 5901 Kissena Blvd. Flushing, NY 11355 rhernandez@magicexterminating.com rhmaestre@verizon.net

May, Dean, BCE, Sr. Sale Representative, Amvac, Plano, TX 214-789-8839

McClellan, Dr. William WDM Consulting wdmconsulting@aol.com

McDonald, Amy President McDonald Marketing Communications, Dublin, TX www.mmcsolutions.com amy.mcdonald@mmcsolutions.com

McFadden, Drew, Sales Manager, GMT Xcluder, drewf@gmt-inc.com

McGuinness, Mike BCE, Technical Director, Entomologist, Interpest, Inc. 678-985-8800 off 678-787-6892 cell www.interpestinc.com

McKnight, Susan President; Susan Mcknight, Inc manufacturer of ClimbUp insect interceptor, 901-848-3831, susan@insect-interceptor.com, www.insect-interceptor.com

McNeely, Scott R. President, McNeely Pest Control P.O. Box 11318 Winston-Salem, N.C. 27116 ph-336-631-9494 www.mcneelypest.com - scottmpc@bellsouth.net

Meyerhoffer, Stephen, President, Ambush Pest Control, Orlando, FL 352-636-6111

Mills, Doug, Mills Consulting Roswell, GA dmills10@comcast.net Morrison, Gordon, Vector Manager, Bayer Environmental Science, Research Triangle Park, www.bayer.com NC 919-549-2535

Mullen, Shawn, Eastern Region US Sales Manager, Bayer Environmental Science, Shawn.Mullen@Bayer.com 201-874-6533

Nepper, Will, Editor, Pest Management Professional Magazine, wnepper@northcoastmedia.com.

Newberry, Chris, Service Manager, Knox Pest Control, Birmingham, AL 205-326-0080 www.knoxpest.com

O'Bryan, Pat, VP Jamison Lawn & Pest Control, 3638 Sumner Ave, Memphis, TN, pobryan@yourlawnpartner.com

Paige, Dr. John, Senior Scientist, Bayer Environmental Science, 328 Indian Lilac Road, Vero Beach, FL 32963. 772-633-8883

Payne, Gene Jr. Service Manager, Genes Pest Control www.genespestcontrol.com

Payne, Hal S. Office Manager, Gene's Pest Control, Marietta, GA www.genespest.com hal@genespestcontrol.com

Payne, Herbert Jr. Service Manager, Gene's Pest Control, Marietta, GA www.genespestcontrol.com

Payne, Herbert R. General Manager Gene's Pest Control & Termite Services, Inc. Marietta, Ga www.genespestcontrol.com

Pearlman, Bennett President, Positive Pest Management, Whitestone, NY, www.positivepest.com, bennett@positivepest.com

Pereira, Dr. Roberto M. Ph.D. Associate Research Scientist; Urban Entomology Laboratory - University of Florida; Gainesville, FL; rpereira@ufl.edu; http://entnemdept.ifas.ufl.edu/sepmc/CVPereira.htm

Poston, Will, President Mattress Safe Cumming, GA www.matresssafe.com will@mattresssafe.com

Redd, Gordon, President, Redd Pest Control, Biloxi, MS www.redd.com 228-424-4490

Reeves, Tommy, Manager, Oldham Chemical & Equipment, Memphis, TN 800-888-5502

Reid, Dr. Byron L. Ph.D. Technical Manager, Bayer CropScience LP, 2 T.W. W.Alexander Drive, Research Triangle Park, NC 27709 919-549-2515 919-491-7531 cell byron.reid@bayer.com

Reidel, Phillip, VP Sales, Atrix International, Burnsville, MN, 800-222-6154 ext. 720 www.atrir.com

Robinson, Tim, Sales Representative, Oldham Chemical & Equipment Co., Augusta, GA 912-687-3114

Schwab, Ron, Technical Manager, Nisus, rons@nisuscorp.com

Sherer, Dr. Clay, Development Manager, Syngeta, clay.sherer@syngenta.com

Silcox, Chuck, Technical Manager, AMVAC, CharlesS@amvac-chemical.com

Skinner, Jim, VP A&C Pest Management, East Meadow, NY www.acpest.com 516-683-8376

Snell, Dr. Eric President/Owner, Snell Scientifics LLC (pest research), 188 Vega Rd, Meansville GA 30256, esnell@snellsci.com , 770-358-4591

Sorkin, Louis N., BCE Entomologist/Arachnologist, Ensult Associates, Inc., Consulting Entomologists, 14 Bobbie Lane, Rye Brook, NY 10573 914-939-0917

Stocker, Robert, National Accounts Manager, Atlantic Paste & Glue, 210-602-4526 www.catchmaster.com

Teague, Joe, Sales Representative, Univar USA, 206-390-6348 joe.teague@univarusa.com

Thomas, Dr. Claude, Ph.D. Sr. Technical Representative, B&G Equipment, Jacksonville, FL

Thompson, Dr. Ray Ph.D. Entomologist, IPM Associates, Inc. www.ipmassociates.com 972-769-2440

Tweedy, Mike, Sales Manager, Rockwell Labs, mtweedy@rockwelllabs.com

Van Istendal, Ed President, EJV Associates, bugsvan@aol.com, 215-292-5844

Viscuso, Lisa, Catchmaster, lisav@catchmaster.com

Walker, Wayne ACE , Senior Pest Control Technician, University of Florida Department of Housing and Residence Education, Gainesville, Florida 32611 352-392-2171 ext 10917 352-284-3963 cell waynew@housing.ufl.edu

Wegner, Dr. Gerry, Ph.D. BCE Technical Director, Staff Entomologist, Varment Guard Environmental Services, Inc., Columbus, OH 43229 www.varmentguard.com 800-793-8169 gerry.wegner@varmentguard.com

Wendell, Bernard, ACE Arrow Exterminating Inc., Lynbrook, NY 516-593-7770

White, Jeffrey M.S. Research Entomologist. Bed Bug Central, Lawrenceville, NJ. www.bedbugcentral.com jeff.white@bedbugcentral.com

Whitford, Marty Editor In Chief, Pest Management Professional Magazine, Northcoast Media, mwhitford@northcoastmedia.com

Whitney, Daniel W. Managing Partner, Whitney & Borgris, LLP dwhitney@whitneybogris.com

Williams, Lance, VP Pest Services Co., Mt. Rainier, MD, www.pestservicescompany.com, 301-779-5800

Appendix V:
About the Authors

Austin M. Frishman, PhD
AMF Pest Management Services, Inc.
Boca Raton, FL

Dr. Austin M. Frishman has dedicated most of his adult life to combating cockroaches. As a pest-management technician, he was profoundly influenced by the persistence of these pests and their adverse effects on humans more than fifty-two years ago. His accomplishments and awards in the field of cockroach and pest management are numerous.

In the 1970s he worked with American Cyanamid as the lead researcher in heading the team that would develop the industry's first successful cockroach bait. The retail product was launched as Combat while the professional product was launched as MaxForce. Both products still enjoy a significant role in their respective markets. Baiting for German cockroach control became a significant change for the professional pest-management industry. With baiting, flushing cockroaches is eliminated, which helps prevent asthmatic attacks in children at infested locations.

Working with certain manufacturers, he introduced the first sticky trap monitors to the pest-management industry, which became a fundamental step in detection and monitoring for pests. Sticky traps have been used to monitor for cockroaches and other pests ever since.

Two separate scholarships in entomology have been established in his name. The Pi Chi Omega Frishman Scholarship provides support to entomology students from this national fraternity of college graduates in urban pest management. The Dr. Austin M. Frishman Endowment Scholarship at Purdue University was announced with great surprise in January 1994 when scholarship founder Paul Bello presented Dr. Frishman with a commemorative scholarship plaque at the Purdue Annual Conference.

On National Geographic Television, "Doc" was featured as Dr. Cockroach. In this show, Dr. Frishman led a team of pest-control technicians through a cockroach cleanout of a commercial kitchen where thousands of cockroaches were killed onscreen. He also appeared in a documentary filmed for *Nova*.

In 1995 Dr. Frishman was awarded the John V. Osmun Alumni Professional Achievement Award in Entomology at Purdue University. He received the Pest Control Technology Leadership Award in 1998. In 2002 he was inducted into the *Pest Control* Magazine Hall of Fame. Dr. Frishman has published nine books, written hundreds of papers on the topic of pest management, has been a member of the Entomological Society of America for more than fifty years, and is a board-certified entomologist (retired).

Dr. Frishman is one of the industry's pioneer independent consultants. His clientele include housing authorities, food manufacturers, pharmaceutical facilities, museums, the US military, and scores of pest-management companies throughout the United States and abroad.

The consummate educator, he has traveled more than three million miles conducting seminars throughout the United States, Canada, the Caribbean, Australia, Bermuda, Brazil, Israel, England, New Zealand, Peru, Japan, Twain, Aruba, Curacao, and Jamaica, and has presented before countless thousands of pest-management industry professionals.

PHOTO 0.5: **Dr. Austin M. Frishman and Paul Bello on the set working together on the Bayer bed bug training video in August 2011.**

Paul J. Bello
PJB Pest Management Consulting, LLC
Alpharetta, GA

Paul J. Bello has been a licensed certified applicator since 1976. He was introduced to pest management by Dr. Frishman and began his pest management career as a service technician working at Suburban Exterminating in Smithtown, New York, while a student of Dr. Frishman's in the Pest Control Technology Program at SUNY Farmingdale. He later enrolled at the University of Georgia where he earned his BSA in entomology. He also holds an MBA in accounting from Adelphi University.

Paul has worked as a technical director for large and international pest management firms and owned and operated his own pest management company located on Long Island, New York, for ten years. His extensive pest control experience led to career opportunities with global basic manufacturers where he served as a technical representative, sales representative and national account manager.

Following in the footsteps of Dr. Frishman, he appeared on the National Geographic TV show *Swarms* where he was featured in segments on German cockroaches and the red imported fire ant. He has been interviewed on many television news broadcasts and appeared in the *New York Times, Newsday,* the *Atlanta Journal Constitution* and other newspapers.

Paul has written numerous articles that have appeared in *Pest Control Technology, Pest Control* and *Pest Management Professional* magazines and was selected as a revision author for the *Arnold Mallis Handbook of Pest Control*. In October 2011 his first book, *The Bed Bug Combat Manual,* was published.

He is the founder of the Dr. Austin M. Frishman Endowment Scholarship at Purdue University and has served as a volunteer and board member to pest industry trade associations. He is a sought-after speaker who has presented before audiences at industry and non-industry conferences across the United States.

Paul is president of PJB Pest Management Consulting and has assisted many clients across the country in resolving various problems including bed bugs, cockroaches, rodents and other pests. His clientele include pest management firms, pest management industry manufacturers, hospitality facilities, theme parks, property management companies, healthcare facilities, public health departments, housing authorities, municipalities and others.

CPSIA information can be obtained
at www.ICGtesting.com
Printed in the USA
LVIC06n2048141213
365092LV00001B/1